MW00417028

The Entrepreneur's Voyage

Rules and Tools for Success in Business and Life

Eliot J. Tubis

To my beautiful wife Julie
and children Nicolas and Justin.
I love you.

© 2008 Eliot J. Tubis

First edition

Printed in the United States of America

ISBN 978-1-60585-396-3

CONTENTS

ACKNOWLEDGMENTS

I am grateful to the many friends, partners, and family members who have contributed to my entrepreneurial voyage. I especially want to thank Patricia Totton, who has been with me almost since the beginning. I want to thank Anne Wayman, Barbara Fifer and my assistant Cathy Muller for helping me finally get this book on paper. I want to thank my beautiful wife Julie for her support and great advice, in life and in business, for her love and for each day we share together. I also would like to thank my children Nicolas and Justin for putting a smile on my face every day and making my life complete. I wrote this book for both of you to inspire you to live your lives on your own terms and live your dreams.

INTRODUCTION

A voyage is a long journey of discovery to a distant land. This is exactly what entrepreneurship offers: a journey full of unexpected adventures and treasures as you navigate your way to a destination that exists not in a place but in your mind's eye.

This book was originally inspired to give my children a road map to understanding business and entrepreneurship. I have tried to keep the book very simple for anyone to understand, yet the concepts and what I call the "rules and tools" you will learn along the way are truly powerful and implemented daily by many of the most successful entrepreneurs in the world. I have tried to keep this book short and concise, the reason being—just like in business—you need to cut to the chase, get the facts, and make decisions quickly and effectively. I hope you enjoy this quick read. I believe the small investment of time needed to read this book will jump start your entrepreneurial voyage!

Lastly, I have changed the names of some of the key players and businesses for privacy purposes.

1

No

Flipping

Burgers!

I grew up in West Lafayette, Indiana—a small college town where Purdue University is located. My dad was a physicist at Purdue, and my mom, who has a master's in biology, also worked at Purdue. Science and academics were at the core of my life growing up because the town revolved around the university. As a kid, I did not know a single business-person. In fact, strange as it may seem, while growing up I had almost no exposure to business whatsoever; strange because so much of my adult life has revolved around creating businesses.

There were some clues along the way. I never felt part of the crowd of scientists and colleagues my parents socialized with and, although I played often with their kids, I always felt a little out of place.

In high school I was at best a B and C student. Academics simply didn't interest me. School felt confining. Sports were more interesting to me, but not the typical midwestern sports like basketball and football. I was attracted to individual action sports like bicycle motocross (BMX) and skateboarding. I was also into weight training because I liked the idea of pushing myself to get stronger and getting in great physical shape.

In other words, I had different interests than most of the other kids in town; it's not surprising I often felt like I didn't fit. Don't get me wrong, I wasn't miserable; I had friends but I felt like I was waiting for life to happen.

No surprise, given my grades, I couldn't get into Purdue in spite of both my parents being on the staff there. Instead, I went to an easier school called Ball State University in Muncie, Indiana and I went to college more because it was expected of me than out of any real desire to study. Ball State's claim to fame are graduates David Letterman of late night TV and Jim Davis, the creator of the cartoon cat, Garfield. Not your typical scholars coming out of most institutions.

Once I was in college, the only classes I had any real interest in were those in marketing and business. That is when I began to think about business and wonder how I could have a company of my own.

My draw to entrepreneurship wasn't just about wanting or needing money; my parents provided me with plenty of spending money. Looking back, I realize that part of the reason I even thought about starting a business was that the whole idea of picking a career path and ending up with a typical job struck me as boring beyond belief. Without understanding it, I wanted a bigger life, with real freedom. I dreaded the idea that when I graduated from college I'd end up in a mediocre job, or, even worse, stuck in some office cubicle. The idea of only two weeks vacation was depressing; I wanted to have my freedom to do what I wanted, when I wanted. I really had a difficult time following the typical path of a college student and, in the end, that is what helped me find unique opportunities to be successful and to live the life I truly want to have.

Lessons Learned While Not Quite Flipping Burgers

Like most kids in my town, I did my share of part time jobs in high school and during the summers of the first couple of years I was in college. Each one of these jobs taught me valuable lessons about myself and about the way the business world works. And each one contributed, in its own way, to my ultimate determination to be a successful entrepreneur.

Detasseling Corn

Since Lafayette, Indiana is surrounded by cornfields it's not surprising my first job, the summer I was fifteen, was spent detasseling corn. The fact that farmers had an exemption, and could hire fifteen-year-olds was part of it; so was the fact that they paid about twice the minimum wage.

Unless you've lived around cornfields you probably have no idea what detasseling is. The tassel on an ear of corn is removed so the corn plants can be crossbred. Before the sun rises, you get picked up with a bunch of other kids in a truck, which takes you to the fields. There, the boss points you to a row of corn. In the early morning, the corn is wet from the dew and you get soaked as you move from stalk to stalk pulling off each tassel, hand over hand, ear after endless ear. By noon, you're dry, caked in mud, and it's gotten hot. You've got to stay covered up to avoid both sunburn and corn rash. Besides, the edges of the leaves on the corn plant are sharp and, without protection, you end up with a thousand tiny cuts. Most detasseling is done in the summer heat, and the rows of corn seem endless. At dusk, the truck hauls you back home and the driver reminds you of how early you're starting the next day.

Sure, I was earning decent money for a kid, but every day was absolutely the same; the intense physical work was exhausting. Unless you've done something like this, you can't imagine how depressing it was to know, at the end of each day, I'd have to get up the next morning and start all over again in the morning. I swear it felt like I was a convict in a chain gang! I detasseled corn only one summer—that was more than enough. Although I didn't know it at the time, this job was the beginning of my quest to find another way to earn my living.

Retail in the Mall

The next summer, I was determined to get out of the summer heat. I went to work for Just Jeans, a retailer who, at the time, had an outlet in the nearest mall; the mall was air conditioned, making it so much more bearable. My job as a junior clerk was to track inventory, make sure the shelves were properly stocked and to sell jeans. In other words, it was a normal job for a teenager. It wasn't awful, but I soon realized I had absolutely no say or control in anything about my job. As low man on the totem pole, I had to work weekends and split shifts. My schedule was totally dictated by even the lowest level manager.

On the other hand, I discovered I was actually good at selling jeans. Talking with customers, finding out what they liked, answering their questions and helping them make choices was fun, and much more interesting than stocking shelves. I was learning how to communicate well and build relationships with people, a skill that would pay off later on.

Still, the lack of control I had over my time and the boring aspects of the job meant I wouldn't go back the following summer. I just couldn't do another mall job.

Dollars and Doughnuts

I don't even remember why I took my next job, but I went to work for Mr. Donut. You don't see the chain around much anymore, but it was about what you'd expect—a small storefront selling coffee and doughnuts. I'd get there about 6 A.M. and, with another clerk, get the freshly baked doughnuts ready for sale. We'd put jelly in the jelly doughnuts, ice the ones that needed to be iced, and set them up in the display cabinet. We also brewed gallons and gallons of coffee.

Again, I had no control over my time. I showed up when I was told to show up; I always worked weekends. The work wasn't hard, but it was boring. After all, it doesn't take much to master filling doughnuts with jelly or making sure the display case looks decent.

The one positive aspect of the job was I really liked interacting with the customers. I was good at it. We had many repeat customers and it wasn't long before I knew what all the regulars wanted. I'd have Mr. Jones' glazed doughnut and coffee with two sugars ready almost as he walked in the door or Mrs. Smith's plain doughnut and black coffee ready by the time she reached the counter. Unconsciously, I was learning the value of customer service. My people skills increased, right along with my unhappiness at these typical jobs. Since the pay (minimum wage) was so low, my paychecks were barely anything.

Working at the Movies

A brief stint as a ticket taker at the local movie theater was not only boring, but also gave me my first understanding of how "office politics" are played. Again, I was the newest employee and I can't tell you how often I watched the manager (who was basically a career ticket taker) switch my shift so he could work with the prettiest girl on the crew, or please some other employee who played up to him.

I was beginning to understand that few organizations gave their employees much authority, freedom or creativity in the jobs they offer. The result was just a lot of misery. I was getting more and more discouraged about the prospect of a so-called "regular" job.

Another Ridiculously Awful Job

One of the worst summer jobs I ever had was working at Purdue in the cafeteria as the person designated to catch the dirty trays and dishes coming off the automated conveyor belt. The job consisted of clearing all the uneaten food, dirty utensils and dishes from the trays, then sorting the dishes into the proper bins for the dishwashers. The stench of all the food and dirty dishes literally made me nauseous. I was caked with food every night and smelled like garbage on my drive home. Needless to say, that was about it for me in the food service industry.

Camping Profits

By the summer of my freshman year in college, I was searching for any way to get into business for myself. I had a couple of ideas, but no plan. Meanwhile, I'd run into this friend from my hometown who had made a lot of money the previous summer selling campsites. I thought it sounded like a great opportunity and asked him to help me get a job there. Within a week, I was in DeMotte, Indiana selling Yogi Bear campsites.

My job was to greet people who had come to visit the campground and receive a free gift. I would then tour them around the site, showing them up to three campsites that were available for sale. Next, I would turn them over to a sales closer. I was paid by the hour plus a commission every time one of the families I gave a tour to actually bought a site.

Everything from what I wore to what I said was carefully scripted. It was up to me to add my personality, and the more excitement I was able to build, the more likely it was the customer would buy. In fact it was amazing just how many people did buy.

It was there I also began to see the power of direct mail. The campground mailed sales letters to families of a certain income level in a 100-mile radius, offering a free gift when they visited the campground. That area included Chicago, so the potential market was huge, and we got a steady stream of people who came for the gift more than any real interest in the property.

The sales process was a well-oiled machine, and I was fascinated, soaking up as much information about the method as possible. I also understood that it was the owner of the campground who was making the most money. He had a product that people wanted and a system to sell it to them.

I was making good money, but I still didn't have the kind of freedom I craved. After all, I had to drive about sixty miles to the campground every day, and spend all day showing the property, then drive another sixty miles home. Weekends were prime selling time, which meant I had no weekends off. I wanted to find a way that would give me both the money and the control over my own time.

It Really Started With Beer Cans

As a kid I had collected beer cans. It was sort of a hobby back then and I'd find them, buy them, and trade for them. I'd then display them in my room and anywhere else my parents would let me put them up.

Along the way, I discovered that the beer distributor in Lafayette had all sorts of items like posters and neon signs that were supposed to go into bars and stores to promote the various brands of beer the distributor was selling. Often, however, the beer sales people never got around to handing out these items. Instead, these advertising items would stack up in the back of the warehouse, gathering dust and taking up room. One day I asked if I could have some of these items and, since they needed to get rid of them, they were happy to give them to me. I thought this was cool because they made great additions to my beer can collection.

Little did I, my parents, or anyone else, know that those beer cans, beer signs and posters would become the basis of my first business.

When I got to college, my parents provided me with spending money, but I loved the idea of making my own money. I hadn't been in my dormitory long that first year when it dawned on me that everyone wanted to decorate their dorm rooms, and the paraphernalia I had gotten from the beer distribution company back home would make perfect additions. Maybe, I thought, I could sell these. I didn't act on this idea until my second year, but my dissatisfaction with all the typical jobs I had, led me to give it a shot.

I looked in the Muncie Yellow Pages and found the area had more than one company distributing beer. Sure enough, it turned out they were as happy to give me promotional stuff as the distributor in Lafayette had been. It really was amazing how much they were willing to give me. I got big mirrors with beer logos, signs that blinked on and off or scrolled the beer name around the frame plus stacks of colorful posters, usually with a female model holding up her favorite brand of beer. I'd drive to the nearest distributor, collect as many posters and signs as I could cram in the car and go from dorm room to dorm room offering them for sale.

All my friends and the other dorm residents were really into beer signs and mirrors; it seemed like everyone wanted something for their room. Since I'd gotten the signs free, I was able to sell them cheaply, and as long as they were willing to offer me something, a dollar, three dollars, five, whatever, every penny I made was 100 percent profit.

Not Always Easy

It wasn't all easy, however. For instance, the second time I returned to the distributor closest to my dorm, the warehouse foreman, who as I remember was a big, and hot tempered Hell's Angels–looking guy, got really suspicious and started staring me down. "You can't just come here and get more stuff," he yelled at me. Needless to say, I didn't go back there for quite a while, but somehow his attitude didn't discourage me. I just moved on to the next closest distributor.

That business grew pretty fast. It got so I was looking in the Yellow Pages for beer distributors all over the state. As soon as I cleaned out one distributor, I'd move on to the next. Before long I was driving long distances to score beer signs and other promotional products. I loved the freedom of making money my own way and that feeling of independence kept my mind racing for more ideas.

In truth, even though I was able to go back to several distributors more than once, my inventory was drying up. In other words, I had no control whatsoever over my product. Although the price certainly was right, I had no way to guarantee a constant flow of product; that's not a good place to be if you want to grow a business.

As time passed, I also began to realize that I could only make as much money as my personal selling time allowed. Yeah, I could get a couple of guys to help, but the beer sign business was really dependent on me. It was hard to delegate anything and almost impossible to duplicate myself, doing it the way I was doing it. As a result, my profits were pretty limited.

While certainly better than the kinds of jobs I'd worked, in many ways my beer sign business was not unlike having a job. I did have more freedom, but to make more money, I had to spend more time knocking on doors. There was a limit to how many doors I could knock on in a day and even begin to keep up with school, let alone have a social life.

This recognition led me to begin to understand the importance of being able to leverage people and delegate. More about that later.

Between the limited inventory and the fact I was restricted to selling only the product I could personally move meant I found myself keeping an eye out for another idea to make money.

Pieces of the Business Puzzle

All that driving around to beer distributors gave me lots of time to think. I realized that my little beer sign business had many of the same characteristics of a much larger enterprise. It dawned on me that building a business was not really as complicated as some so called "experts" want to make it. **I began to realize that, in its simplest form, a business is buying something for $1.00 and selling it for $2.00, and then figuring out how to sell a whole lot of it. If a person could sell 1,000,000 items at a $1.00 profit each, they could make $1 million!** I also recognized that my beer sign business had two fundamental ingredients that were common to most successful businesses.

Your product or service must be something lots of people want and it also should have a very high profit margin. The bigger the profit margin, the better.

That's not to say a company cannot be highly successful without high profit margins; however, a large profit margin allows a business owner much more room for error. I personally have no interest in low margin businesses. There are just too many pitfalls that can kill a thin margin business overnight.

It hit me that a lemonade stand that kids set up on a hot summer day was not fundamentally different than huge companies like Coca Cola™ or Microsoft™. Both of them have a product with high profit margins that lots of people want. In spite of the problems of limited inventory, my beer sign business was like that. As this realization hit home, I began to get very excited because I could see the puzzle pieces coming together in how to be in business for myself.

I was determined to figure out how, using these two simple concepts (high profit margins plus a product customers really want), I could stay out of the normal workforce and make a lot of money. I was beginning to see that if I could become a successful entrepreneur, I could control my own destiny and have real freedom. I just hated the idea that some day I might get stuck in a dead end job somewhere with little control over my time or the amount of money I made. I'd tasted the freedom of being an entrepreneur and loved it.

I also began to understand why I felt so out of step from the people around me. To keep my beer sign business generating money and to figure out my next move, I really had to be thinking all the time. My mind would race on, night and day, about how to deal with a problem or opportunity, or how to expand my business. I loved that excitement.

I read all kinds of books on business, listened to motivational tapes, asked questions of every businessperson I could manage to meet. I was like a sponge trying to soak up as much insight as I could. As it turned out, I think this hands-on approach to learning to be an entrepreneur was much more powerful than taking a class or analyzing some case study. Doing something in the real world is the best way to learn.

Meanwhile, my friends were just out having fun, barely thinking about the future, just kind of going with the flow. I knew most of them would end up in run of the mill jobs, and follow the typical career paths that most parents and educators push.

Now, some twenty or more years later, I really can see clearly that when you add the compounding of time, money, and experience into the equation, my life and freedom are so unbelievably different from those of most of the kids I grew up with. Many of them are still struggling to get by and have almost no real freedom or financial independence.

Sometimes it was hard to be different from the crowd, but I wanted a better, more exciting life so I made a pact with myself not to follow the crowd for comfort's sake.

I continued my beer sign business through my junior year at college, but I knew I had to find another business as a replacement for it if I really wanted to make some real money.

2

STUDENT
EXAM
SURVIVAL
KITS

At the beginning of my senior year in college, I started brainstorming on all kinds of business ideas. I experimented with screening crazy slogans on T-shirts, and although they sold fairly well, the whole process took up way too much time for the small profits I earned. Then I remembered a great idea from the days I lived in the dorm.

I recalled how one day, as we were all studying for semester finals, my roommate got an exam survival kit from his parents. It had all sorts of snacks—mostly no-name candy and stale granola bars. Even though the contents of the box were pretty bad, I thought it was a cool idea and was even more surprised to discover that most of the kids living in dorms on campus were getting them—about one out of every three students. At that time I never really thought about the concept of survival kits as a business, but it finally dawned on me that this could be a great little business to get into.

I did some research and found out that a company in Boston was marketing survival kits to parents nationwide. Just prior to finals, they sent parents letters offering exam survival kits for their college kids to help them deal with the stress of cramming for tests.

It was truly a great idea, but the execution was terrible. The snacks were off brand and junky; no one really liked the contents, but all the students loved the idea of getting the exam survival kit. After thinking it through, I knew in my gut I was looking at a real opportunity.

One of the things I thought made the business so interesting was the fact that all the sales would be done through the letters to parents. This was so much more efficient than going door to door, as with the beer signs. The power of the letters would be like having a huge sales force go to each parent's home. This reminded me how great the sales letters worked to get potential buyers to come see camp sites at the Yogi Bear campground I had been working at a few summers before.

I could see that the parents, particularly the parents of freshmen, were worried about their kids who were away from home for the first time. Not surprisingly, many of these parents wanted to do something extra to support them during exams. I decided I wanted to go into the student survival kits business, but do it in a first class way.

The feeling I got that told me this idea was good is what I call a "gut feeling," meaning my intuition was screaming, "hey, this is a great idea." I have learned over the years how important it is to listen to your gut when making a decision. If you really tune in to your brain and body you can usually "feel" the right decision. By listening to your gut, you will make faster and better decisions. It's great to analyze and study information to help guide your thinking, but don't forget how important tuning into your gut can be.

Use your gut—learn to make decisions and correct mistakes quickly by using your gut and trusting your feelings.
Feel the right decision and go with it.

One thing that's almost always true about starting a business is that there will be lots of challenges along the way. No business is problem free or easy. What makes the difference is how you solve the problems that come along.

The first challenge was to find parents' addresses so I could send them a letter offering a survival kit for their student during the next final exam period.

I started asking around the campus and it turned out my friend who was on the student association board had access to a list of the students' parents, complete with mailing addresses. He was happy to provide it to me. Fortunately, the list was broken down by class so I could tell who the freshmen were; the address told me how far away the parents were from campus. I figured that the farther the parents lived from the college, the more likely they would be to send a survival kit since they probably didn't see their child that often.

Finding Initial Funding

Almost every new business needs a little money to get started, and mine was no exception. I went to my parents and described the exam survival kit business I wanted to start. Intuitively I felt I should do a small pilot test-mailing to about 500 parents and that I should mail my offer to only those parents of freshman who lived 100 miles or more away from the campus. I wanted to do a test mailing because, although I knew the idea was great, I really didn't know how it would all work out. My parents agreed to loan me enough to get started.

One of the real advantages I had is that my parents were truly supportive of my efforts. Even though they were both academics and didn't know a thing about starting a business, they were always there with a helping hand.

That money covered the cost of mailing a professionally printed sales letter, brochure and gift card that the parents could sign and return along with the $15.00 I'd decided to charge for each kit; I would enclose the signed card with the survival kit when I delivered it. The cards provided a nice personal touch.

A friend helped me sort through the mailing labels over Christmas vacation.

Remember, this was back in the mid-1980's, before everything was computerized the way it is today, and we were dealing with paper stick-on mailing labels. We sorted out the parents of freshmen and I sent off the 500 letters. It didn't take long for checks to start showing up in my mailbox. The first thing I had to do was open a business checking account.

Of course, once the checks started rolling in, I had to put together the kits for each student. Using the Yellow Pages again, I found a candy wholesaler in a nearby town and ordered hundreds of candy packets, granola bars, and other items—all recognized brands and all fresh. I also tracked down wholesalers for the other things included in the kits like little "Do Not Disturb, I'm Studying" signs for the dorm door. (Parents loved those!)

I used the checks the parents sent with their orders to finance the munchies and the boxes used to make the survival kits. The wholesaler delivered all the snacks to the front porch of the small apartment I was sharing with four other guys near campus and I began to assemble the boxes and deliver them to the students on campus.

My test mailing proved the concept was a good one. Testing simply means doing a small test marketing effort to see if the product or service you are offering can be sold profitably. We will cover this in much more detail later; however, it's important to note that by mailing just 500 letters initially, I was able to keep my expenses to a minimum while seeing what the true interest in the survival kits was. Ironically, I tested simply because I didn't have the money to mail more solicitations anyway, but I believe testing business concepts at low cost is one of the most powerful tools in business. I made a decent profit and was able to pay my parents and my expenses with some money left over.

I took the money I'd made from the first round of mailings, after paying for the candy and boxes and postage, and immediately mailed more letters. It only made sense to me to reinvest my profits to create more. It was tempting to run off and spend it, but I was determined to make my exam survival kit business grow.

Some Goals Achieved

When it was all said and done, I realized I'd gotten about a 15 percent response rate. That's an unheard of return on a direct mail offering. Typically, a response rate of 1.5 or 2 percent, and sometimes less, is considered a great success. By the time I'd finished, I'd mailed a couple of thousand letters, and ultimately sold about 400 exam survival kits. Yes, I personally filled most of those boxes myself (my roommates did help from time to time). And yes, I personally delivered each and every one to the dorms on campus where the kid receiving the package lived.

I'd also succeeded achieving a major goal. Although there were some problems with this system, I had managed to move completely away from the idea of a single sales person knocking on doors. By creating sales letters I'd discovered how I could radically increase my sales with minimal effort. Almost without realizing it, I had created a successful direct mail business.

Like my beer sign business, I had a product that people wanted; unlike the beer sign business, I could control my inventory—as long as I had money to pay for the contents of the kits, I wouldn't run out of product. Not only that, I had a product that customers, the parents, wanted and were willing to pay for and pay a high enough price so I made a good profit on each sale.

The exam survival kit business had the two most critical elements of any successful business: A product with a very good profit margin, and, most importantly, a product that customers (the parents) wanted.

I'd also come to understand that much of what was going on in the classroom was really aimed at teaching students how to earn a living, with the emphasis on getting a good job. I didn't want a good job. I knew if I could get the right systems in place to expand I could make a lot of money. I got excited about rolling exam survival kits out to more and more campuses.

Bootstrapping—Another Piece of the Business Puzzle

Although I didn't know it at the time, I'd also discovered the advantages of bootstrapping a business. Bootstrapping is starting and growing a business by pulling the business up from nothing. It's done by reinvesting profits from early sales and only building out infrastructure and employees as the growth comes. This is the opposite of many venture-capital based companies that raise a bunch of money from investors before they have any real product development or sales.

Bootstrapping allows you to own the entire company.

There are two problems inherent in the venture-capital based model. First, in order to raise the funds, the entrepreneur has to give up a lot of ownership, often most of it, to attract the investors. Secondly, having a large pot of money makes it tempting to spend on all kinds of nice-to-haves like posh office space, expensive cars and high-paid employees, which don't necessarily help the business to grow or be profitable.

There are huge advantages in bootstrapping a business, which include:

- **Bootstrapping forces a you to start selling on Day 1.** You have to be totally customer focused and serve that "want" we discussed in Chapter 1. This allows the business to be profit focused immediately.

- **Bootstrapping makes you be frugal and not waste money.** Businesses that raise a lot of capital tend to burn money on unnecessary equipment, marketing, and people that don't really drive the business forward. Bootstrapping makes you stay absolutely focused on spending money only when there is a clear and direct benefit.

- **Bootstrapping makes you cut through the clutter and just starting selling and making money.** There is no build-out of a big infrastructure nor is there a huge, long payback time when you bootstrap. You eat what you kill—meaning you make sales to make money! Don't let anyone fool you: business is selling, first and foremost. Nothing else really matters in business if you don't have customers and profit.

- **Bootstrapping forces you to be creative and use unique ideas to create opportunities and solve problems.** This leads to building a stronger company that can survive and thrive in good times and in bad.

- **Bootstrapping allows to you own all or at least much more of the business.** The wealthiest business people in the world realize how important it is to own as much of a company as possible so that, when it becomes highly profitable and valuable, you don't just get a small sliver of the profits. By staying lean and bootstrapping, you can hold on to a larger ownership stake.

- **Bootstrapping gives you freedom because you owe no one anything.** By bootstrapping, you don't have investors or a venture capital company to answer to. You are your own boss and have the flexibility to run things your way.

- **Bootstrapping is rewarding.** Creating a business from nothing is exciting, fun and can also make you a fortune.

Learning About Delegation

In the meantime, while setting up the survival kit business, I was taking a full schedule of classes, and part of the class work was writing papers. In those days, papers were typed on a typewriter, and typing was not a talent of mine. Fortunately, there were people who advertised typing services on the campus bulletin boards. I hired a lady named Tracy to type papers for me, little knowing what a good decision that would turn out to be. One day I showed up at her house to pick up a paper and I must have looked wiped out because she asked me why I was so tired.

I explained about the exam survival kit business I'd created and complained about how hard I was working at stuffing envelopes to send out the sales letters and getting the kits I'd sold together for delivery.

She lit up saying she'd like to make extra money and offered to set up an envelope stuffing operation for me out of her house. It turned out Tracy was a dynamo. She hired some other homemakers and I paid her something like a penny per stuffed envelope. This was perfect, because by then I'd started to expand by getting lists of parents from all the other colleges and universities in the state. I had a lot of envelopes that needed stuffing.

Business delegation is created when functions of a business are performed by other people or by a process so that the delegator does not have to do the work themself.

Working with Tracy taught me my first lessons in delegating to others. Delegation is a fantastic tool to fuel growth and profits in a business. I was the marketing guy, and hiring her and her friends meant I no longer had to deal with the initial mailings because I had turned it all over to her. It wasn't long before they were also helping me fill the survival kit boxes for just a few cents per box.

From Front Porch to Warehouse

One day the manager of the wholesale candy business I was buying all the snacks from knocked on my door. I'd bought so much from him that he wanted to find out more about what was going on; he said he wanted to be sure I wasn't setting up another candy wholesale business in Muncie that would undercut his.

When I showed him what I was doing, he was impressed with the idea, but thought I was nuts trying to do this all from my apartment. He had only to point to the stacks of boxes and piles of snacks to make his point.

It turned out he had extra warehouse space and suggested that I use that space to fill the boxes and stop shipping all the candy to my apartment. He didn't charge me much rent because it actually saved him money and hassle on delivery. I went for it. Tracy also loved it. It meant she could set up a real assembly line and get the mailings out and the survival kits filled in much less time with less effort.

The move to the warehouse also meant I could expand my mailings to even more colleges and universities. I decided to add Purdue to my list of schools since it was in my hometown and I could easily find some friends to help me deliver all the kits there. Again, I had a buddy who was on the Purdue University student council and he agreed to provide the list of parents in exchange for a cut of the profits for the student organization. Today we'd call this a joint venture.

As it turned out, that Purdue list was the most responsive ever. My exam survival kit business was really taking off. That first Purdue list also led me to make my first major mistake.

A Hard Lesson

The following semester, my Purdue friend was replaced on the student council and the new student in charge wasn't interested in doing business with me. Looking back, I think his decision was based on his understanding of how much money I was making from that list. He couldn't see any reason the student organization couldn't do it all themselves, making much more than the percentage of profits I was paying them.

Instead of renegotiating or just letting go of the idea of marketing to Purdue parents, I talked my friend into getting me the new list through his own sources and mailed my offer to those parents. I hadn't thought through what might happen when the student organization mailed a similar offer to the same list. Not surprisingly, the parents, who had gotten two letters offering exam survival kits, started calling the university asking what was going on and which was the "real" letter.

As soon as the parents started calling the university, Purdue started calling me. To say they were upset understates the problem I had unwittingly created. Purdue, of course, felt it owned the list of parents. They wanted to know how I had gotten a list and, before long, they filed a lawsuit against me, accusing me of unauthorized use of their list of parents.

I had to hire a lawyer and eventually cleared up the mess; the suit was dropped, but it turned out to be an expensive and humiliating lesson that would have ramifications for years and years.

Don't step into any gray area in business—
it will usually end up being trouble.

You should try to look at all business decisions as either black or white, meaning black means don't do it; white means it's okay. If you are not sure, still don't do it! Gray is what gets people in lots of trouble.

My exam survival kit business kept growing in spite of this bump in the road. I became extremely careful about how I acquired the mailing lists from that point on.

My business was successful beyond my wildest dreams. In fact, by the end of my senior year, back in the mid-1980's, I was making about $70,000 a year.

Even so, I followed through with some interviews with a few prospective employers—that was, after all, what all my classmates were doing. And I did get a couple of job offers from companies that were impressed with my marketing ability. Of course, they were offering annual salaries of around $12,000 to $15,000, which was considered decent money in those days. Are you surprised I turned them down? I couldn't believe I was making five times what they were offering with my little survival kit business.

I returned home to my parents' house and took the summer after graduation to figure out how I would continue to expand the business in the fall before final exams rolled around again. Remember, I'd done all this from an apartment and a warehouse. I'd never had an office. Although Tracy was handling fulfillment, I didn't have any other support systems in place, like a secretary or a bookkeeper. All I was sure of was that I wanted the business to become bigger and better.

3

Partnerships

Are Like

Marriages

After a couple of months of kicking back and thinking at
my parents' home, I rented an apartment in Indianapolis and
began gearing up for the fall mailing. Tracy was still on board
and we refined both our mailing and our survival kit packing
systems. I also hired a part-time bookkeeper to help me keep
track of the money.

And I bought both a condo and a Porsche which, considering
how much money I'd made, didn't seem outrageous at all. Let
me say now that spending your profits on flashy cars and other
material things before you're truly rich is a sure path to disaster.

Following our previous formula, that fall Tracy and her team
mailed more than 200,000 letters to the parents of freshmen in

over 100 colleges and universities in the Midwest. As the checks arrived, she'd order the snacks and other items, fill the boxes and address them. Obviously, I couldn't hand-deliver every package any more, so I'd have them sent to the student's dorms by mail and, initially, that worked out fairly well.

Sometimes, however, the delivery was bungled because the dorm staff wouldn't deliver the packages to the individual rooms, which meant some remained in the mail room. As a result, I was investigated by postal inspectors who wanted to make sure we weren't running a scam. Luckily, I was always able to prove my good intentions for the delivery of each and every package and avoided a potential disaster. Although the postal authorities were satisfied, the fact that they had even investigated would come back to haunt me later.

A Partnership Begins and Ends

Then an odd thing started to happen. I began to get orders for another company selling their own exam survival kit packages as well as orders for my own. I was getting mail intended for a company with a similar name located in Cleveland, Ohio! That company was also sending letters offering survival kits and the parents were mixing up the checks and order forms.

I called the owner and we straightened out the confusion. As we talked, we realized we had many of the same goals and ideas for business expansion. We formed a partnership for a huge mailing, aimed at May and final exams at colleges and universities around the country.

Although we were about the same age, the owner of the other company had a better understanding of business systems and processes than I did. It was his idea to go to facilities that work to find jobs for disabled workers, and hire them to put the snacks in the boxes as the orders came in. This was much cheaper than paying Tracy. That was fortunate because Tracy about had a nervous breakdown as the business got bigger and she was totally burnt out. She was working almost 24/7 and needed a break.

Greed Kicks In

I'm still not sure just why, but I started ignoring my instincts and gut about which parents to send letters to. We decided not to limit our mailings to the just parents with freshmen who lived about 100 miles from the campus. Instead, we mailed to all the parents of all the students, freshman through seniors, even if the student lived close to their parents.

This was a totally new approach. Remember, before even starting the business, I intuitively felt parents of freshman were much more concerned about their kids and by the time a student was a sophomore or older, the parents would think the students could handle finals on their own. I also thought parents who lived farther from their kids were more likely to send a survival kit. This time I ignored my instincts; I got greedy thinking mailing to more customers would results in bigger profits. That was a big mistake!

The truth is I got excited and started counting potential profits instead of really thinking rationally. My thinking ran something like this:

"Our product cost is cheap, so even if a smaller percentage of parents order, we'll still be making a ton of money. If we mail more; we're bound to make more money."

If only that had been true.

We mailed to something like 3 million parents! By then, we'd hired a huge mailing house that automated the stuffing, stamping and mailing of envelopes. That mailing cost about $800,000—not exactly small change. Remember, we'd done no testing to see if broadening our target customer mailings would work.

It didn't take long to realize we were in trouble. Timing in a business like ours was both critical and revealing. You couldn't send an offer too close to finals because there wouldn't be time to process the orders. On the other hand, you couldn't mail months in advance either, because the parents would forget all about it. As a result, the mailing goes out all at once, about six to eight weeks before final exam week.

Because of the timing, the orders start coming in right away; the orders did pour in, but we weren't tracking things well enough to realize that the response rate was way down. In fact, there were a lot of orders and at first we congratulated ourselves about being smart enough to order a ton of snacks in advance to get a great price; we'd based that order on the close to fifteen percent response I'd been receiving by mailing to the parents of freshmen only. It turned out that I should have listened to my "gut" and instincts. Parents of sophomores, juniors, and seniors turned out to be way less likely to order exam survival kits for their kids than the parents of freshmen. Our response rate fell like the proverbial rock—it was less than half of what we'd projected.

Money and Reputations Lost

By the time we filled all the orders we did get, we'd lost more than $200,000. It was a mess. Because of my previous successes, my credit was excellent and I had signed purchase orders for almost everything personally, which meant I was on the hook for it. (This type of personal guarantee turned out to be another big mistake; I'll talk more about this later.) I owed the candy wholesaler, I owed the mailing house, I owed employees—it seemed like I owed everyone. I should have tested the concept of expanding our target market to parents of all students. If I had only tested mailing to just 1,000 to 2,000 parents across all grade levels, I would have realized how much lower the response rate of parents with students in the higher grades was and this could have saved us from losing hundreds of thousands of dollars. So, one more time, the rule is **test everything**.

Testing is the process of running small pilot programs to see if a product or service can be sold profitably. Almost any business concept can be piloted on a small scale to gauge its success. By always testing, you'll never lose a large amount of money—best of all, testing allows you to quickly sort your losing concepts from your winners. Once you find a winner, then you can put additional time and effort into expanding them rapidly. In short, kill your losing tests, but massively expand your winning ideas.

Test everything! By testing you protect your downside (meaning how much you can lose) while also learning how much upside (profit) you are creating. The simple rule is: Test everything!

I used up all my savings to pay for the postage for the huge mailing. Ultimately, I gave the mailing house a lien on the condo I had bought about six months before. I sold my Porsche, not only to raise money to pay debt, but because cruising town in an expensive sports car when you owe serious money only makes things worse. We worked out a deal with the candy wholesaler and paid him fifty cents on the dollar. In fact, although it seemed to take forever, I finally got everyone paid off.

In a single year, I'd gone from having a direct mail business that worked and gave me a significant income (around $70,000 per year) to a disaster. I was close to broke. My credit was ruined.

It drove me nuts because I knew that if we'd only tested expanding the mailing to all parents, we would have avoided the disaster because we would have discovered the response rate was way down. But we didn't. We didn't stick to basics and allowed greed to do our thinking for us. Needless to say, part of the unwinding of the business was the dissolution of the partnership with the guy from Cleveland.

Cash Is King

Another business lesson I learned while going through the survival kit disaster is a simple rule "Cash Is King." What this means is never come close to depleting your cash reserves, in both your business and personal life. When you get low on cold hard cash, you and your business can't help but start behaving in a desperate manner. Having a good cash cushion always allows you protection when things go wrong and gives you firepower to take advantage of opportunities.

It's not easy, especially starting out, to have a large cash cushion, but it should be your first priority in both your business and personal life. In the early days, it means keeping expenses low, being cheap, and negotiating every purchase.

One way to create discipline around cash management is

to sign every check yourself. This allows you to review every transaction so you have a close eye on all aspects of your business and personal expenses. Once your company gets to a large size, you can set parameters such as you sign all checks over a certain dollar amount. This still allows you to track the pulse of cash management even as the company grows to a large organization.

Other Valuable Lessons

During these early years I learned some other very valuable lessons, including:

- **Find a good CPA and lawyer.** Before starting any business, find a good Certified Public Accountant (CPA) and business lawyer. Later in the book I will talk more about surrounding yourself with smart mentors, employees, friends and advisors. The reason I mention the importance of having a top notch CPA and lawyer is that they can help you structure your business as a corporation, which protects your personal assets from creditors if the business cannot pay its bills. The CPA will help you to keep your tax bill as low as possible. Over time, you will learn that if you are successful and make lots of money, taxes will be far and away the largest expense you will have. A good CPA and lawyer could save you millions over your business career. The best way to find a top notch CPA and lawyer is through referrals from highly successful business people and mentors. Always look to successful people for advice, rather than just hiring someone who is a "friend" of a friend. When it comes to your CPA, lawyer, and doctor, only accept the best.

- **Don't Personally Guarantee Business Loans.** You always want to avoid personally guaranteeing a business loan because if the business can't pay it back, the lender can take your home, savings, or any asset you have. You might have to find a different lender, but there is always a way to finance a business without a personal guarantee by being creative.

- **Weekly Flash Report.** One of the simplest ways of keeping a good handle on the financial position of the company is to prepare weekly "Flash Reports." A Flash Report is simply a report that tells you "in a flash" the basic health of the business. At minimum, the report should show:
  1. Cash position of the company
  2. Accounts Receivable (what money is coming in)
  3. Accounts Payable (what money you owe)
  4. Sales Pipeline (what sales are projected over the next week)
  5. Income Statement (weekly and year to date)

Every company needs to customize the exact data that they look at, but bottom line, you want to be sure the company is generating positive cash flow and can easily pay its expenses.

Charlie O. Finley

As I was licking my wounds from the failed mailing, an old girlfriend of mine introduced me to Charlie O. Finley, the former owner of the world champion Oakland A's baseball team. She was working for Charlie in Chicago as his executive assistant. At the time, Charlie was around seventy years old and was a colorful character. I told him a little about my business, and he was impressed at my energy and enthusiasm. It turned out he had made his fortune in direct mail insurance and then went on to buy several sports teams.

The direct mail connection and his success gave me hope that I could resurrect the survival kit business. I thought about asking Charlie to be partners in a new version, but I just couldn't do it. He was more valuable as a mentor and a teacher. I spent several weeks just hanging out in his office, as he loved to teach young entrepreneurs about how to succeed in business. His mantra was S + S = S. This meant:

Sweat + Sacrifice = Success

Even though Charlie had a reputation as an egomaniac and heartless baseball team owner, he gave me a glimpse of inspiration to figure out how to persevere and relaunch the business.

Find a mentor/or mentors—entrepreneurs who have already made it big love to help others succeed. Don't be afraid to ask a successful entrepreneur to mentor you.

Partnership Number 2

I began looking around and brainstorming about how to get the survival kit business started again. Meanwhile, another friend of mine told me that her sister, who was a waitress at a business hotel, had met a wealthy businessman who was looking to invest in businesses. I agreed to meet with him.

It turned out I was meeting with John Rollins and his partner. They were stereotypical, cigar-smoking business operators. Rollins was in his late fifties then; I was in my early twenties.

Rollins was a character, to say the least. He started his working life as a school superintendent but had always been interested in business and active in local politics. Along the way, he'd acquired an interest in a tiny rural bank in a small Indiana town. He used the bank for lots of wheeling and dealing around the state.

I wasn't sure exactly what to expect from such a meeting, but I ended up telling him about my failed exam survival kit business. I didn't pull any punches, explaining both what had gone wrong as well as what had worked. I discussed with him how I'd do it differently and how I'd avoid the mistakes I'd made.

He was intrigued; in fact he was so interested he offered to loan me $100,000 to start the business all over again.

Now, I didn't do any research or due diligence on Rollins. Due diligence means doing a background check and finding out as much as you can about a person or business. I was young, naïve and, the truth be told, I didn't know about due diligence. Besides, I was dazzled by his offer. If I had done my homework, I would have discovered he had less than a stellar reputation. His business ventures often ended up as disasters, but his contacts often rescued him. He was a mess, but a great mess since he was willing to make a spur-of-the-moment bet on me!

A few days later I went to the bank, and sure enough, there

was a check for $100,000. There were also a bunch of legal papers for me to sign, and I did, almost without reading them, and certainly without much understanding. In essence, we set up a corporation where I got 50 percent ownership and so did he. We named the corporation Student Care Services, Inc. I signed over to him half the business we were starting; in return, he loaned me the money. He didn't invest or put up any of his own money; I was on the hook for the loan from his bank.

A New Exam Survival Kit Business

I began to build the new exam survival kit business. We were careful to mail only to the parents of freshmen, testing everything, and the business started to take off. The survival kit idea was a winner again. In fact, Student Care Services and the kits ultimately became the platform for every business I've created since. There were, however, some more major bumps along the way.

The first problem was the partnership I had with Rollins. His reputation and his actions constantly threatened the business. He was always trying to bring one crony or another into the business, or get me to agree to use the business as security for a shaky investment. Sometimes it got crazy. I had to learn how to forcefully say no, over and over again. Fortunately, since I did own a full 50 percent, I could stop him. But it was a constant hassle and by the end we were barely speaking to each other.

In truth, if I'd done any research on the man I probably would have avoided the whole arrangement. About the only smart thing I did with him was, after a couple of years, insist he sign a buy/sell agreement.

One of the problems with business partnerships is that things change. One partner wants to move, or gets sick, or something. The buy/sell agreement sets out the rules of how one partner can buy out another. Part of ours included life insurance policies on each of us to the tune of five million dollars; he was the beneficiary of my policy and I was the beneficiary of his. This way, if either of us died, the other would have enough money to buy the partnership from the estate. This sort of agreement is just one of the many must-haves for any partnership, none of which I knew about in the beginning.

We went on like this for years. The business began to make serious money. Rollins would take his profits and invest them in some other business, one that would usually fail. That, however, kept him mostly out of my hair.

Eventually, he died of prostate cancer. I was able to use the funds from the insurance policy to finally, not without some legal battles, buy the company.

Partnerships Really Are Like Marriages

Although I'm not opposed to all business partnerships, my experience has certainly led me to be cautious of them. Like marriages, partnerships are easy to start, but not so easy to maintain. Differences of opinion between partners are bound to happen, sometimes huge ones. It's amazing just how much give and take is needed if the partnership is to survive and make money. The improper action of one partner can damage the reputation of the other. It can get worse than that. One partner can literally destroy a business if things aren't handled properly.

In addition, there has to be an exit strategy for every business partnership and it needs to be written down in contract form. It's not as simple as it looks, not by a long shot.

Cheaper To Hire

Usually, it's cheaper, over the long haul, to hire people than to partner with them. When you're dealing with an employee, the rules are much more straightforward. And if you have to fire someone, you can if they are an employee.

Some argue that partnership is a better arrangement because the partners have ownership and therefore will work harder or more efficiently, or more creatively. I've found that it's possible to give employees the same sense of ownership with a good bonus structure or profit sharing arrangement. That's what I do with my key people; it's worked great for me. Profit sharing allows your top employees to share the wealth and success of the business. I discuss this more in the chapter "Building a Team."

4

OUTSTANDING
STUDENTS
OF AMERICA

In spite of the problems with the partnership, Rollins and I continued and, by many measures, we were successful. That first fall, through Student Care Services, we offered the exam survival kits to a carefully targeted group of parents. Our criteria were based on my original success—parents of freshmen who lived 100 or more miles from the college campus. It worked and our response rate was back up to around 10 to 15 percent.

Vulnerability

Although we were successful, we really had only one product, the exam survival kits, and those could only be sold two or three times a year, depending on the final exam schedules of the various colleges and universities. That made us vulnerable. After all, I'd already run into one competitor and it wasn't beyond a possibility that someone else would surface and make an offer that would compete with ours, reducing our response rate and therefore our profits considerably. Besides, we had the infrastructure in place, with the mailing houses and the facilities for disabled workers who did the packing set up, but it wasn't being used year-around.

As a result, in our second year we began to add to our product line. For example, in October we offered a Halloween treat box; in February a Valentine's Candy selection, etc. There was also a Fruit Basket, a giant tin of gourmet popcorn and even a Home Style Birthday Box complete with cake.

Although the response rates on our other products never matched the original exam survival kits, because we were careful to test and to target, we made a good profit on each of these items. This created not only a large income, but it came in year around, and we were able to make more efficient use of our infrastructure.

There Are Rarely Totally New Business Ideas

Another of the hidden truths about business is that, by and large, there are no absolutely new ideas. Almost always, a successful business is started not with a new idea, but with a creative adaptation and/or improvement of an old one. Growth in almost any business often comes from, if not copying, modeling on what someone else is doing—but doing it better. You don't have to look very far to find examples:

- Bookstores certainly weren't new when Jeff Bezos launched Amazon.com, the world's biggest web-based bookstore. His innovation was to move what we now call a brick and mortar store to the World Wide Web.

- Henry Ford didn't invent gasoline-powered engines. They'd been around for almost a hundred years. He didn't even invent the assembly line; he was simply the first to do it well enough to make cheap cars available to the masses.

- Microsoft certainly wasn't the first software developer, nor was Apple the first to develop a portable music player, and Domino's wasn't the first pizza delivery company.

The list could go on and on. In each case, someone recognized a product or a service that had potential and developed it in new ways that maximized profits. The trick is to stay open to seeing existing products and services in new ways. By taking a business concept and putting your own personal stamp on it to make the product or service truly unique and innovative, you can create your own successful business.

Another New Idea Drops In

We'd solidified our expanded business and were generating profits year-round when a friend of mine mentioned he'd gotten a direct mail piece from a company called Who's Who Among College Students. I realized this had to be a huge money making venture when, once my friend was accepted into the program, they sold him a very expensive certificate of membership and an equally expensive directory of honorees.

Over the next few days, I began to understand just how much profit potential was in a Who's Who type business. I also recognized that our mailing list for exam survival kits was perfect for a similar Achievement program targeted at students in high school and college. I began to do some research. Remember, this is before the days when you could simply Google an idea. I spent a lot of time in libraries looking at books, magazines and trade publications.

I discovered that there were many different versions of Who's Who or Achievement recognition companies. Each had developed different audiences and criteria for membership. Some targeted high achieving business people, others targeted students, teachers, etc. There were all sorts of variations. Once a person was accepted, they were offered directories with their contact information, achievement certificates, plaques of acknowledgment, and other items for a high price.

Each had a different target market, but they all worked about the same way. Although some of those aimed at students offered scholarship money, it was in relatively small amounts. The truth was that ego gratification was the name of the game. I began to wonder how I could add real value to the concept.

I found an issue of *Entrepreneur Magazine* that advertised business plans for sale. One of these was a plan for Who's Who type businesses, which cost only $49.95. I ordered it and it had everything I needed to begin, including templates of actual letters I could adapt and send to parents of college students, letters congratulating students on being accepted, etc. The templates were great but I still hadn't found a way to move out of the simple, ego-driven, name recognition business into something more useful and unique.

A New Spin

My parents were a major part of our success. Remember, they were academics with little experience in business, but they always supported my efforts. When I showed them my friend's Who's Who directory, they were quick to spot it had little utility on its own and was, in fact, more about vanity than anything else. It didn't take them long; however, to help me see how the directories could be improved. They had a real understanding of what universities needed when it came to recruiting students, and it was largely due to their input that we divided the graduates into categories by their majors. Once we had the categories, it became obvious that many organizations and universities might find this information useful.

We next decided to distribute the categorized contact information for free to companies, organizations and universities who could make use of it by contacting graduating students in the majors they were interested in. For example, universities and colleges could find the right kind of candidates for their advanced degree programs; an aerospace company could look for engineers and find graduates and soon-to-be graduates to approach with job offers; companies needing marketing staff could find students who were marketing majors, etc.

Distributing the categorized information free didn't cost us much, but it made our offer much more attractive to our prospective customers—the students who would soon be graduating from college and high school. By joining our program, their names would be in front of the very people they were trying to reach, automatically. Not surprisingly, our ability to alert companies, universities and other organizations about outstanding students through our categories was a huge selling point to our students.

We set up a strict application process to make sure our students truly were outstanding. We added scholarships in large amounts that would be awarded to qualifying students on the basis of their academic record, their extra-curricular activities and an essay they wrote. Again, my parents helped. In fact, they (along with one other person), read the thousands of essays and actually chose the scholarship winners. Without their understanding of academics and ability to recognize the most outstanding students, our program would have been less effective. Ultimately, we were awarding over $100,000 in scholarships each year.

We made sure our directories were not only categorized, they also looked impressive with leather-like bindings and raised gold lettering. Our other products were of first class quality also, so people didn't mind paying the high price we charged.

By now I swore by test marketing every offer and after some fine tuning, figured out how to make our offer work really well. Soon we rolled the program out across the country to millions of college students.

By the end of our second year, Outstanding Students of America had become an enormous success. Organizations like the State of Connecticut's criminal justice department, Eli Lilly, Honeywell and the Department of the Navy and many,

many others quickly discovered that the categorized contact information for students we gave them free was of tremendous help in recruiting employees.

We expanded our offering to high school seniors and it wasn't long before colleges and universities found our information provided real assistance in recruiting students for their programs.

How It All Fit Together

The business was actually straightforward. We'd send a letter and brochure to students offering membership in Outstanding Students of America. The first letter described the application process and made it clear that the contact information of the qualifying students would be distributed to companies and colleges. We charged a $5 application fee, which covered our initial expense; if an applicant failed to meet our criteria, we'd return their application fee.

Accepted students were sent a copy of their biographical information as it would appear in the directory for editing and/or approval. We had a roomful of data entry employees keying in the information that, once it was correct, would be published in the directories and set up as lists for distribution to education and hiring organizations.

Another letter offering the directory, certificates and plaques would go out to students, parents and eventually, even grandparents, of accepted applicants. Of those who ordered, 40 percent purchased about $50 worth of product—a directory plus a plaque or a certificate. On our mailing to grandparents, we got about a 20 percent response rate so we had the opportunity to sell tens of thousands of directories, plaques and certificates to grandparents as well.

Our costs for the directories, plaques and certificates were extremely low. This made OSA a great business because we had products that the customers really wanted, which we were able to sell with extremely high profit margins.

We easily sold 150,000 directories, and 200,000 certificates and plaques, one of the reasons we were able to give away about $100,000 in scholarships each year.

Success Brings Problems

Our success also meant we posed a real threat to those companies already in the student recognition business. Because we were able to offer true value through the free distribution of the categorized information, and because we flooded the market by sending out millions of applications to apply for membership in OSA, they were seeing their profits decline as ours grew, and they didn't like it one bit.

It always amazes me when competitors try to win by attacking rather than by improving their own product or service. They could have easily adapted our innovations and become real competitors; instead, the decided to fight us.

First they put into place a set of "industry standards." I put this in quotes because, in truth, the standards were written by one company and designed to benefit that company only. Their business model was different from ours. Instead of asking students to make application, they sent mailings to teachers and asked them to make nominations of top students; they would then market the directories and other items to the nominated students. So one of the standards they tried to impose was: acceptance into a student recognition program could be by nomination only. Their standards didn't mean anything; there wasn't even a trade organization for student recognition programs, let alone anything like a standard in the industry.

The Past Comes Back To Bite

Not surprisingly, the competitor also started to research Outstanding Students of America and the owners, Rollins and myself. Of course, they found the record of the investigation the U.S. Postal Service did of me and my original survival kit business. They also found innumerable references to the questionable business practices my partner had engaged in over time outside our partnership.

Although Rollins never had been convicted of any crime, he was, without question, a wheeler-dealer. He had to defend himself against many lawsuits, often making settlements to get the matter dropped. All this was, of course, public record.

And the company trying to sink us ignored the fact that the U.S. Postal Service had cleared me of all charges.

Our competitor took this partial information and ran with it. They contacted various states' attorney generals and, using their phony industry standards and newspaper reports of my troubles and Rollins's problems, convinced several to start investigations. They also filed suit against us and began a campaign my attorney said went on record to say was "…the most vitriolic campaign to eliminate the competition I have experienced in my thirty-two years of practicing law."

They accused us of all sorts of things, including failing to return the application money to students who weren't accepted (not true; we returned every cent and could prove it) to including students who didn't deserve to be included (also not true and again we could prove it). The situation was terrible.

As a result, we began to spend enormous amounts of money and time defending ourselves, even though not only had we done nothing wrong, we were offering a better product than anyone else was in the marketplace. When the dust settled, I had a collection of letters and stipulations from the various states involved admitting that we had done no wrong and that our services were valid. But the effort finally drove me out of the business. I'll talk more about how that happened in the next chapter.

There are many lessons here, but one of the most important is to see how a new door opens even when you might be in the midst of a failure. I would never have entered the most profitable part of my business life without first starting OSA. Keep reading and you will see what I am talking about.

Reputation Is Extremely Important

It's hard to over-emphasize just how important your reputation is in business, and I came close to losing mine. Sure, the problems started over stupid innocent mistakes in college. But the accusations were enough to cause real problems later on. Over and over again I've had to defend myself; I've always won because my mistakes were honest and I took immediate steps to correct them. My business life, however, would have been much easier had I thought through some of my earlier decisions more carefully.

This is brought home even more dramatically when I recognize that I never did the right kind of research before taking on Rollins as a partner. If I had, I might not have done it the way I did. Again, we were able to defend ourselves and Outstanding Students of America because we hadn't done anything wrong at all, but it cost us financially and emotionally.

Your reputation is built over a career and can be lost in a moment. Work hard to protect it; you'll be glad you did.

Don't do anything that you don't want on the front page of the newspapers, because it could easily end up there.

5

RECURRING REVENUE—
ONE OF THE
REAL SECRETS
TO WEALTH

In spite of my own failure to protect my reputation, and in spite of the problems I encountered with Outstanding Students of America, that isn't the whole story. For it was Outstanding Students of America that put me in the perfect position to create an entirely new business that was extremely profitable and also created a massive recurring income stream.

Recurring Revenue

Businesses that have recurring revenue tend to be highly profitable. Recurring revenue, also called residual income, is created when a business continues to generate income as customers use your product or service, over and over again. You actually continue to make money on a regular basis even though you are doing no more, or very little additional work. In fact, ideally, you won't have to do any continuing work and the money will still pour in.

Musicians and actors who continue to receive residual income from broadcast performances years ago are an example; so are book authors who receive royalties long after they wrote the book. The banks and financial institutions that issue credit cards are another example—every time you use your credit card, they make money. They also earn money while customers are sleeping because the interest accrues on loans day and night.

As you know by now, I've always been on the lookout for additional business opportunities. This was intensified as my discomfort with defending OSA continued. Because OSA was really a mail order business, I was always immersing myself in every book on mail order I could find. One day I was reading a book called *Inside the Leading Mail Order Houses.* There I learned about a company called the National Marketing Group (NMG), located in Boston, one of the pioneers in the affinity credit card industry.

An affinity credit card is a credit card that's branded with both the credit card name, like MasterCard or Visa, and with name and/or logo of another, sponsoring, organization, often a charity, like Ducks Unlimited, or the Sierra Club. The banks love these deals because they get access to highly targeted mailing lists and have the implied endorsement of the sponsoring organization. The sponsoring organizations love affinity cards because they get a percentage of every transaction. The broker who puts the deal together, in this case NMG, also gets a percentage.

As I thought about this, I knew I had a list of over 200,000 members of Outstanding Students of America. Every one of them was graduating with a B grade average or better, and they would soon to be looking for and starting their first jobs. It seemed to me they would make an ideal target market for an affinity credit card.

I set up an appointment and met with NMG President Joseph Binder and his partner; together, they had already made hundreds of millions of dollars with affinity credit cards. They were enormously wealthy business people and their offices almost blew me away. The conference room not only had great views of Boston but electronic white boards and state of the art computers I had never seen before. Everything about their offices and staff was impressive.

Binder and his team saw the potential of the OSA members right away. My hunch was right on; high achieving graduating students were exactly the kind of market they were looking for. As we talked, they explained to me the potential of the affinity credit card market and I realized they understood the value of my targeted membership list far better than I did. Effectively, they told me I was sitting on a gold mine. I was seeing dollar signs in my head!

A few days later, they introduced me to the one of the largest credit card issuers in the country at the time, and we cut a deal that looked like this:

- The bank would put together the credit card solicitation letter and send it to every member of OSA.

- The bank would pay all mailing and marketing costs.

- I would get $25 for each and every application they approved.

- I would also get 20 cents for every transaction made, forever, on all the cards they issued through this program—true residual income.

When we signed, I had no idea just how lucrative this would turn out to be. Essentially my only contribution was the list of members. Of course, I had worked hard to develop that list, and now it was now a highly desirable group of potential customers for the bank.

By the time the controversy around OSA was at its worst, we were receiving checks up to $500,000 each month from the credit card deal. We consistently were getting a 7 or 8 percent response on the mailings; most of the applicants were approved, putting lots of money in our pockets, but the real payoff came as the card holders used their cards. Twenty cents per transaction on everything from pizza delivery to gasoline purchases adds up in a hurry.

It wasn't long before NMG asked us to experiment with telemarketing to sell the credit cards to OSA members. We first tested the concept by outsourcing to a local state-of-the-art call center. We discovered that we could improve the response rate to a full 50 percent of every person reached by phone. That's right; every other person we called applied for one of our credit cards. Compared to the 7 or 8 percent response from the mailings, it was almost unbelievable. Obviously, we began to move from direct mail to telesales immediately. The firms we used to make the calls to our members utilized computerized telemarketing systems so the representatives offering our cards never had to dial at all; they just talked to one member after another. This process was so efficient and cost effective that it made our telemarketing profitable from the first day.

Recognizing a Stepping Stone to a Huge Opportunity

Our membership list, of course, was of top students only. This was great, but the list only consisted of the 200,000 OSA members. We still had the contact information for all 5,000,000 students on our database who were not OSA members, and I realized this was a huge untapped source of additional revenue.

We had become experts at sourcing information about college students. Again, remember this was before personal computers made compiling lists fairly easy. We'd created a system to gather information on students from all over the country. We hired data entry personnel to key in names, addresses and school information on millions of college and high school students. This database could then be sorted by all kinds of criteria such as years in school, phone number, etc.

Our bank partner wasn't interested in expanding their credit card offering beyond the OSA members so I started looking around to see if I could find another bank who would issue credit cards to students who were not members of OSA. Essentially, what I did was find a directory of the top fifty credit card issuers and started calling them. I'd explain that I had a proprietary list of several million students that would make ideal candidates for their first credit card. I was turned down over and over again. Although I was sure the market was there, my approach wasn't working.

Another key to business is to be willing to change what you're doing when it isn't working. It took some thinking, but eventually I found an approach that worked. Instead of just pitching the list, I packaged it into another membership program. It worked like this: the sales letter offered membership in an exclusive student-purchasing group. The benefits of that group included a credit card along with other benefits like discounts at major retailers, scholarships, auto insurance and student loan information.

Presented this way, another one of the largest credit card issuers in the nation loved it. Of course, in addition to finding a better way to package our list, I also had to find out a great deal about making presentations to large sophisticated banks.

One of the reasons we were successful at landing both banks was our preparation and planning for our meetings with them. Our team rehearsed and brainstormed on every potential question or concern these banks might have. In the end we came across so polished and professional they almost could not say no. This is where plain old hard work and preparation pay off.

When our team met with the new bank for our pitch, we truly had all our ducks in a row. As a result, I was able to cut a deal with them that was similar to the deal with our first banking partner. We named this new membership program Career Images and soon we were mailing and calling as many college students as we could find. Our ability to constantly source new student information became an integral part of what we had to offer. In fact, our database group would eventually compile an updated list of phone numbers and addresses on all 5,000,000 students each year.

Hitting the Jackpot

To our amazement it turned out our telemarketing response rate was roughly the same 50 percent when we tested the Career Images credit card program and before long we were outsourcing those millions of solicitations to call centers throughout the country. We quickly had over 1,000 telephone sales reps in six different call centers, working seven days a week.

Leveraging People and Technology

The marketing power of these thousand reps coupled with the efficient calling technology of the computerized dialers allowed us to generate huge profits almost overnight. It blew me away to sit in my office and realize that while I sat there a thousand reps were making sales for our company and I didn't have to lift a finger!

We had a staff of database managers for each call center we worked with. These people made sure the centers always had the optimal list of students for the best sales performance and made sure every center had enough prospects so they never had to stop calling. It was a science to keep feeding good prospects to each center and monitor all the performance reports to make sure we were generating the highest number of sales for the lowest cost possible.

Every penny we saved on our customer acquisition cost went into our pockets so we watched everything like a hawk. Remember, we got paid $25 per approved account, which meant if we could book an account for $10 we would clear $15 profit up front per sale. On top of this, we still earned the 20 cents per transaction on each card for as long as it was used.

High Profit Margins and a Simple Equation

The profit margin was a simple formula—it cost about $25 per hour for us to hire one telesales rep. That included not only their salary, but the infrastructure to support them—the computers, the support staff, the facility, etc. When a rep sold two approved credit cards an hour, that created $50 in revenue per hour; subtract our $25 cost for that hour and we cleared a profit of $25. It worked out that we were calling over 2,000 hours on many days, which meant we were making up to $50,000 a day in profit!

As our credit card business became highly successful, I realized that OSA was just a stepping-stone to get to the real gold nugget in the business, credit cards. Working with our banking partners, the credit card business became extremely profitable. This business required no inventory, had recurring revenue, and no competitor was giving us any hassle.

Letting Go of the Old

Once I was convinced our credit card marketing efforts to all students was paying off on a regular basis, I made the decision to shut down OSA; it was draining my time and energy because of all of the controversial issues and accusations that were being thrown at us. It happened this way:

One day, driving back home with my attorney following a long meeting defending OSA, including showing an attorney general all our records, testimonials, and other information, I turned to him and said, "Enough! I'm getting out of this business."

He thought I was nuts. Not only were we making several million dollars a year, in every case we had been successful at defending our reputation. I was, however, tired of the fight and had begun to realize there was a better way to make money.

Nevertheless, it's important to realize that without starting OSA and building its member base, we would never have entered the credit card business. This is an example of why it's so important to just get started with a business concept and let the opportunities unfold as you grow.

I haven't had a major controversy over my business since I let go of OSA. I'd learned my lessons. I've been asked why I didn't sell OSA. It's possible I might have been able to, but it was time to simply let it go, to walk away from the problems and let my new business carry me.

All business plans are very rough outlines—just start, don't be afraid to swing the bat. Begin with a simple concept and let the rest unfold as you power your way forward.

6

BUILDING

A

TEAM

Every successful entrepreneur has to learn to delegate if they really want to succeed in a big way. It's just impossible for one person to handle every important issue or decision in a fast growing company.

I learned this lesson by trial and error. As the company grew, I always had a couple of go-to employees to help me execute a project or business idea. However, in the early days, I didn't have anyone who could make the necessary strategic decisions or who had the ability, let alone the authority, to operate the company and take the business forward. As a result, for several years I was working eighty-hour weeks; even when I wasn't at work, I would still be thinking about the business, usually late into the night.

The pace was crazy. I started to gain weight by eating tons of candy from the survival kits in the warehouse every time I got nervous. (I have a habit of eating when I get nervous!) I had very little time for a personal life and even though I was making quite a bit of money. I felt anything but free.

Surround Yourself with Smart and Creative People

Business owners must surround themselves with the smartest associates possible. This means both inside the company with employees, and outside with friends, mentors and professional resources. I mentioned earlier that almost every business has been built or created by modeling the achievements of others. By surrounding yourself with the smartest people possible, you will not only learn from them but inevitably be helped by their creativity and brainpower.

As a personal example, I have been a member of YPO (Young Presidents Organization) for over ten years. Founded in 1950 with the mission to "create better leaders through education and idea exchange," the organization currently has some 11,000 members in ninety countries. YPO has been a fantastic resource for entrepreneurs, CEO's, and business owners throughout the world. YPOers, as they are called, know the power of surrounding themselves with other like-minded people, and the relationships that develop can be unbelievably rewarding, both personally and financially. My YPO relationships have been the single most important resource of business support and growth outside my family. I can't stress enough the importance of surrounding yourself with the smartest and most creative people you can find.

Who Owns Whom?

One day, feeling completely overwhelmed, it finally hit me that I needed to do something differently. The business owned me; I didn't own the business. As I always say, "If you have to be there every day, you have a job, not a business." I had to make a change. I needed top-notch leadership in the company, or I or the company was going to explode.

> **Build a team with shared
> vision and goals—hire
> team players who are leaders.**

One of my big problems was that I loved creating the ideas but really didn't have the patience or skills to execute them well, down at the detail level needed. I'd learned this back in the survival kit days and fortunately was able to surround myself with a few key people that helped me get by.

As I was realizing I needed to find some real help, I got lucky. I actually found the person I so desperately needed to help me sitting ten feet from my desk: my assistant, Patricia Totton. Patricia actually was Rollins's assistant when I first met her. Rollins offered me the opportunity to pay her salary so that she could work for our new company. In very short order, I realized she was extremely smart, intuitive, and had the energy and drive to expand our business. Patricia was the silver bullet I needed to keep the business and myself on track!

Patty started out as a kind of Jack (well, Jill) of all trades, helping in almost every area of the company. Quickly she moved from being my Personal Assistant to Vice President, then Executive Vice President and then to the Head of Operations. After a few years of working together on every aspect of the company, I finally stepped back from the daily decision-making and let her run the show. We worked very closely and at the end of every business day we would meet to go over the day's events and key issues the company was dealing with. This is where I found I was able to excel. I became the idea guy and the sounding board to discuss important strategic decisions the company was involved with while Patty handled the details.

Delegate and Monitor

I do believe when you do delegate, you have to monitor the results of the team very closely. I call it Delegate and Monitor. You are not doing the work, but you are watching all the results on a real time basis. This is the only way not to be blindsided by unexpected events.

Just about the time that we started marketing our credit cards, I had turned over all the operations to Patricia and had made her president of the company. I felt a huge sense of freedom and relief. This gave me the ability and time to travel and have a social life, while still monitoring the business closely. It also gave me the opportunity to get out of the trees so that I could see the big picture.

Finding a way to see the big picture is very important. It allows you to look out to the horizon to spot new opportunities so you can continue to formulate the vision for the company.

I do believe the vision of a business is created, shaped and maintained by the founder/entrepreneur for a long period of time, and that this is a very valuable and necessary contribution. Creating and expanding the vision of the company is not something that can be delegated easily. As an entrepreneur, you need to have what I call think time.

You need to get out of the trees—You need
at least one hour a day to think strategically
and get out of the trenches.
This is where "Vision" comes from.

Think Time

In fact, it's impossible to think strategically when you're fighting fires; you need calm. Carving out think time is another reason to delegate as much as possible!

After about a year of this newfound freedom, I did the unthinkable. I walked into the office and said to Patty, "I am moving to California!" I promised that I would come back whenever she needed but that I was ready for a life change and wanted to move out west. It is something I had always wanted to do, but never had the freedom or financial means to do it until that moment.

Now, some fifteen years later, Patty and I still have the same routine of checking in every day at 5 P.M. eastern time to go over the day's events. I also do this with key executives in some of the other businesses I have interests in. I have learned that I never want to be an operator, only a combination of owner-entrepreneur-investor so that I can have the freedom to be anywhere and not deal with the day to day business operations. I truly believe if you have to be at your business every day, you're not really an owner but an employee, even if you own the company. Delegating the key leadership roles in the company is what gives you the freedom to call yourself an owner.

Another major criterion of mine when it comes to building a team is: **Hiring is always cheaper than having partners.** We discussed this earlier; having partners is like a marriage. Never bring on a partner just to get a job done. You would be giving up way too much freedom and equity in a company to do this. The only time to ever bring in a partner is for substantial financial backing—otherwise go it alone. This way you will be your own boss, and don't have to be second-guessed or need approval from a partner.

A Lean and Mean Culture

Another key to building a successful team is what I call developing a lean and mean culture. The leader and senior team determine the culture of the company. Lean and mean could be summed up as watching every penny, negotiating every purchase and running with the leanest quality staff necessary to execute your plan.

So many companies, particularly startups, get in trouble because they overspend. It's tempting to buy the latest and greatest computers even when you don't need them. The same thing is true from everything from office furniture to stationery. It's also true of employees. Pay only as much as you need to pay to get the right talent.

Always create a culture of running lean and mean in good times and in bad. Make sure every employee lives by this concept. By doing this you will always stay competitive and be prepared to deal with the unexpected events that can rock a company.

Fat and happy will kill a business every time!

My Hiring Criteria

I am going to be very blunt and give you my exact criteria for hiring and firing people. This may seem cold but after more than twenty years of dealing will all kinds of employees I am going to save you a ton of grief and problems by laying it straight out for you.

Hiring competent people is the key to building a great company. The problem is that it's actually very hard to figure out who the right people are before you hire them. In fact, I believe the best ratio a manager can achieve is one in every three people you hire is worth keeping; the others will need to be let go. A normal ratio is more like one good hire out of five!

I know this is hard to believe, but you have to understand that when people apply for a job, they always put on their best appearance and charm. It's next to impossible to figure out what you are getting until after they are working for you. Yes, you should always do a background check and call several references before you make a hire, and those will help, but the bottom line is you have to be prepared to fire people and fast.

Hire slowly, fire quickly.

The motto is: *Hire slowly; fire quickly.* Bad employees are like parasites in any company; if you don't get rid of them, they spread! Bad employees range from those who spread rumors and misinformation about the company, to those who steal money, trade-secrets, customer information and more. What is even worse is that these types of employees usually recruit other employees to take part in their destructive behavior. This can spin out of control in no time if you don't have a proactive plan to deal with problem employees immediately. For a chart to help you sort out which employees to keep and which to fire, see the table on page 74.

Terminating Employees

You absolutely need to follow all the state and federal laws related to employee rights when terminating an employee. It's best to have a good Human Resources manager who can dot the i's and cross the t's when it comes to employment related matters. The safest thing to do is give people a trial working period with your company to see how they work out. Don't sign employees to long-term employment agreements.

Take Care of Your Team

On the other hand, remember your great employees are the ones you will want to reward with high compensation, a great profit sharing and retirement plan. Great employees are worth jumping through hoops to keep happy!

Profit sharing will align your interests with those of your employees—by giving your employees a percentage of the profits, everyone will be focused on the same goals.

By sharing with the team, everyone is motivated to make large profits as well as to keeping the company running lean and mean!

Reward both yourself and your team when you win. This might mean a big party for your employees, a great trip or a big bonus. Make it fun for yourself and your team when you win! Employees don't work at a company strictly for a paycheck, all of us like to have fun and a sense of accomplishment in our work. Make your work environment a place everyone in the company enjoys.

Celebrate success!

Fire These People Immediately	Keep and Reward These People
1. Anyone with a drug or alcohol problems who refuses to get treatment. Even the most talented executives cannot make good decisions when addicted to drugs or alcohol.	**1. People who are positive.** People with positive attitudes will help the company persevere through the tough times. Positive people find a way to win.
2. People who can't manage their personal lives. We all have problems but you can't take them to work.	**2. People who thrive on change and challenge.** Business is always changing and you need a team that is adaptable and persistent.
3. Untrustworthy people. Once someone breaks your trust, fire them; if you can't trust someone 100 percent, you can't trust them at all.	**3. People who love responsibility.** You need a team of leaders to build a great company. Leaders love responsibility.
4. People who are constantly negative. People with negative attitudes kill a company, period.	**4. People who are critical thinkers.** Critical thinking is a requirement to find opportunities and solve problems.
5. *Yes* people. You need people who will give you straightforward feedback and criticism; if they always say yes they are worthless.	**5. People who are hardworking, honest, and smart.** These people are the foundation of any great company.
6. Greedy people. You know the type; they always want more, more, more. More compensation, more ownership, stock options, more time off, etc. If someone is not excited or motivated by the challenge of the job itself, they are not worth having on your team.	**6. People who share your vision for the company and are leaders.** Your team has to all be pulling in the same direction. Without a shared vision, the company does not have a clear direction and usually fails to achieve its goals.

7

CALL CENTERS—
A FREE BUSINESS!

We continued to outsource all our telemarketing to other companies for about three years. Once we had a good handle on managing all the call centers and on the massive database compilation efforts, our team got curious about how much profit these call centers we were outsourcing to actually earned. We also began to wonder if we could do an even better job of selling credit cards ourselves if we operated our own centers.

We did a lot of research and determined that it wouldn't be that hard to set up our own call centers and it could probably save us a lot of money. We decided to go for it with a test center. If it worked, it would not only give us complete control of the sales process, but it would also significantly increase our profits by squeezing out the profit margin that the outsourced centers were earning.

On the surface a call center doesn't look too complicated, but it turns out that to run one properly requires attention to an amazing amount of detail. I was lucky to have Patricia orchestrating the entire build-out and staffing at our first call center.

Moving to our own call center meant our company would be quadrupling in size, from 50 to over 200 employees, since the call center would require more than 150 reps and managers. Then there was the whole business of the credit card application quality. Each application had to be filled out completely or it would be declined for lack of information. That meant adding an entire quality control department where people read each application taken by the phone reps carefully. When there was missing or unreadable information, and that happened more than you might think, the Quality Control personnel called back students to get missing information. The details seemed never-ending. Patty had assembled a fantastic team of veterans from the call center industry to make it all work. I just sat back and watched it all unfold; that's the beauty of delegating and having a great team!

That first center had sixty-four seats, a relatively small center by most standards. But it was an excellent test bed. We opened using the most advanced predictive dialers. Essentially, a predictive dialer is a computer that dials each call for the sales agent, and monitors the calls in such a way that it can predict when the next agent will be available. It saved enormous amounts of time and increased the productivity on the call center floor significantly.

Patricia was amazing. Not only did she get our first call center running well, but over the next few years, we opened six call centers with more than 1,500 employees. Soon we were able to bring all our credit card sales in house. It turned out that our instincts had been right; we were able to save a huge amount of money compared to outsourcing, and we were getting a much better close rate, which caused our profitability to soar even higher.

Sometimes It Flattens Out

It took several years, but after a while it became obvious that we had more or less maxed out selling affinity cards to students. The business was steady, but couldn't grow because there are a finite number of new college students each year. We'd honed our databases so we were literally contacting almost every student in the country and saturated the market. Competitors also started taking note of our success, and copied our telemarketing process. This made it a race each year to see who could get to the student first. We became very efficient and were usually first to call a student, but the competition became very intense. The only students who didn't have a credit card were incoming freshman so we really ended up in a situation with a static market that we couldn't grow any larger.

To move into selling credit cards to the general adult population seemed a logical next step, but it turned out that most adults already had many credit cards and there wasn't nearly the demand for the credit cards as there were with the students. There was no reason to fight an uphill battle and push a product people didn't want or need.

The other problem we were facing was customer attrition. If 100 people accept a credit card, by the end of a year, only about 80 of them will still have the card. People are always trying new cards, they switch cards, they decide they don't want yours any more; it happens all the time. So even though we kept issuing new cards, our business stayed the same size. We could pretty much maintain our royalty stream, but there wasn't much room to grow. Over time, we knew we had to come up with some new opportunities or the business would slowly shrink.

I kept looking for other ideas and opportunities. I loved the excitement and the challenge of building a bigger, more profitable company, so I just kept searching for our next big hit.

Nothing new seemed to work. We test-marketed all sorts of products from life insurance to mortgages. For one reason or another, nothing we tried seemed to be right for us. We were still making money, but we hadn't yet found a way to grow to the next level. Of course, it's not unusual to have new things not work. It was frustrating, but we kept searching and testing.

One of the most important things about testing is to find out what doesn't work. It also keeps you from losing a ton of money while you find the next gold nugget. We now had a system to protect the downside while looking for opportunities.

The Business We Already Had

Finally, it dawned on us that we already had a business we could grow—the call center business. Just because we used our call centers to sell credit cards didn't mean they couldn't be used to sell products for another company. We began to focus our efforts on finding other companies that needed call center services. We added a division named TeleServices Direct (TSD) to reflect our new focus on finding clients who would outsource their call center business to us.

With Patricia and her team handling the operation and sales, we began to get new clients with different kinds of products and services they wanted us to market. We were able to be profitable even with small clients, because each of our call centers was run in a lean, efficient manner. We didn't spend tons of money on facilities, but instead found opportunities that let us grow cheaply, often by taking over the lease, complete with equipment, from someone who had spent themselves into bankruptcy. That included the predictive dialers as well as all the other office equipment. We didn't rush out and buy the newest computer systems, but found bargains in used equipment. As a result we were able to offer our services at a considerably lower rate than many others.

The Next Big Break

In 1997, I got an update on my daily management call that included the information that we had landed a small contract with a satellite TV provider. Little did I know the opportunity that would create. Initially they wanted to use us to test small programs so they could refine them. We had that ability. Over the next few years, we began to handle more and more of their business, growing from a couple of hundred thousand dollars to over $15 million a year. That led to other huge contracts with some of the world's largest companies.

It's worth noting that a major part of our success in landing the contracts with new clients actually came from our success with managers who had worked with us at their prior companies. Many times these companies were bought by larger organizations and we were able to get new contracts from the bigger parent companies.

> *Cultivate and maintain*
> *long-term business relationships.*
> *These relationships often will*
> *help you over and over again.*

This is how relationships in business often work. The person you treat well today just may be the one who moves up the ladder and/or over to a new company and into a position to help you down the road. Of course, the opposite is true also. That's why it's so important to develop and maintain business relationships as you go along. You just never know how they may help you later on. Today, TSD performs more than 1,500,000 calling hours each year for Fortune 500 companies in both domestic and offshore facilities.

Following the String and Finding the Opportunities

Remember, TSD was a business that we had already built for our credit card marketing efforts, so creating the outsourced call center business really was free of cost to us. Now this free business has generated tens of millions of dollars in profit.

Of course, the credit card business came from following the string from the Outstanding Students of America, and that had come from the exam survival kits, which, if you go back far enough, came out of the beer can business. You'll see the thread is there. Each opportunity unfolded from the one before it. Of course, I couldn't see these growth opportunities up front, and you probably won't either. But they're there—that's why you have to just get started, swing the bat and go for it! You can't hit a pitch you don't swing at. Remember, now that you know how to test and protect your downside, you can never completely strike out. This is really the secret to success in business, the opportunity to keep swinging the bat until you hit a home run!

8

BE THE BANK

Much of the mid-90's was spent settling into a California lifestyle, and making sure TSD was working smoothly even though I was now living 2,500 miles away. My delegation and monitoring systems kept working well, even at that distance. Although things were going fine, I was still on the hunt for my next big opportunity.

Before I moved out west, Patty had told me about a small, privately owned bank in South Dakota called Bank Pacific. They wanted to hire TSD to market some of their credit cards, but they wanted to work with us on an hourly basis, without paying us per application or giving us any royalties. About all we knew was a marketing company selling credit cards to students had purchased the bank. We decided to accept their business and it wasn't until I was driving across the country that I began to wonder about this bank and how they made money off the cards we sourced for them.

As usual, I went on a fact finding mission to learn more about their business. I called the South Dakota banking regulators and found out their credit card business was not only profitable, but growing like crazy. I knew much of their profit was coming from the accounts we generated, but I really didn't know anything about banking or how the credit card industry worked as a whole. I knew about how credit cards were sold—that, after all, was much of our business and we'd done a good job. Our profits were based on the rather simple equations of marketing the cards. But the financing, the banking behind the credit cards was a mystery to me. I began to get intrigued but I hardly knew where to start.

Learning About Banking

Meanwhile we kept testing new ideas and kept getting less than great results. One day, more out of frustration than anything else, I called a big law firm and asked what it would take to set up a bank to issue credit cards. They told me about the seemingly innumerable requirements, like having a CEO who had been in banking at least ten years, and needing $10 million in funding, and qualifying for FDIC insurance—it seemed overwhelming.

By 1996 it was obvious that Bank Pacific, which had started small, was onto something, for they were becoming one of our bigger clients, issuing something like 100,000 credit cards each year. I liked the fact that in their business model, they owned the whole customer relationship and were generating a large income from all the interest and fees they charged on the credit cards themselves. I knew there were large profits to be made but still didn't understand the details. I was determined to figure it out.

One of my fellow members in YPO was a guy who was in the banking and auto finance business. I set up a lunch with him to learn how the banking and financing businesses actually worked and to see if it would be possible for me to set up a bank to issue the student credit cards.

He was impressed that our company had been sourcing millions of credit cards for others and thought we had a real shot to expand into issuing our own cards. He introduced me to his accountant, whose firm specialized in financial services. Because of this contact, I was able to meet with the head of KPMG's financial services division. KPMG is one of the largest accounting, tax advice and business consulting firms in the world.

Other People's Money

The head of their credit card division explained briefly that if we could acquire credit card customers for between $10 and $15 each (I knew we could do this because we were already doing it for others), this would be an incredible strategic business advantage because most banks were spending literally hundreds of dollars to acquire a new cardholder. He also explained to me how to structure the business so that the money students borrowed on our credit cards could actually be funded from a low interest bank credit line rather than with our own money. This would allow us to generate a huge profit, also known as an interest spread. The example he outlined was something like this:

1. Our credit card company would charge 20 percent interest to credit card customers.

2. Our credit card company would fund the cardholder loans by borrowing money at 5 percent interest from a credit line.

We would also have the expense of sending out the monthly credit card statements, customer service, and finally credit losses. (Credit losses are the monies that are never paid back by cardholders who default.) The accountants figured all of the expenses would add up to another 10 percent of the credit card interest we were getting, so the final profit would look like this:

+20% Interest from cardholders
- 5% Cost of borrowing to fund credit card loans
-10% Operational costs and losses
= 5% Net Interest Profit

Now here's the best part—at first 5 percent profit may not sound like a lot, but this was after borrowing all the money we loaned out. This was just like generating a 5 percent interest rate on a huge savings account of someone else's money! Imagine if you could get all the interest on someone else's bank account that had $100 million in it. We would loan out millions of dollars to students through our credit cards, and we'd fund those loans from a very low interest credit line, then pocket the difference and use none of our own money to do it! Even better was the fact that, as the accountants explained, I would not have to personally guarantee the credit line, because the student credit card revenue would collateralize the line. So bottom line, we had limited risk, and huge profit potential. This was an equation I liked!

OPM (Other People's Money) Is a Form of Financial Leverage

I had heard the saying "Use other people's money (OPM)" before, but never understood its true significance. Now the difference in using OPM was clear. If we had to use our own money to make the loans in the same example, we would be investing $100 million to make a small profit, but if we used someone else's $100 million, we would be getting a huge return because we would make $5 million off almost no investment of our own—all we were investing was our database of students and the low cost of generating new customers.

Leverage is the ability to exponentially magnify business profits through unique business processes and financial structures.

Four types of leverage that can supercharge a business are:

1. **People leverage.** Example: I had over 1,000 people selling credit cards for me and I didn't have to do anything except count the money we were earning from all their sales. People leverage is a form of delegating.

2. **Technology leverage.** Example: I had the predictive dialers, computers and a massive student database that allowed our company to make more than 25 million calls per year. Without technology, this would have been impossible. The technology leverage increased our profits by huge amounts. Technology leverage can help create

massive efficiency and scale in a business.

3. **Product leverage.** Example: we offered a product, credit cards, which had a high profit margin and a huge demand from students. Every sale of a high profit margin product is money in your pocket. Product leverage is the combination of the profit from each sale coupled with the volume of sales.

4. **Financial leverage.** Example: We generated much higher profits by using borrowed money (OPM or Other People's Money) to fund our credit card loans. This increased our returns tenfold. Financial leverage is very powerful and must be managed carefully to protect your downside risk.

I was so excited about what I learned from KPMG, that when they offered to help put a business plan together so that we could start issuing our own credit cards, I jumped at the opportunity. That business plan wasn't going to be cheap, it would cost me $50,000, but because I could see the potential, my gut told me it was worth the risk. After all, Bank Pacific had done it without the powerful strategic advantage we had.

A strategic advantage is a unique quality that your business has, which is very hard for a competitor to duplicate. It could be a product, a process, or a cost structure that allows you to beat your competition. Every business needs a strategic advantage in order to thrive and profit.

We knew we had a strategic advantage in TSD. TSD was a credit card sales machine we could use to generate millions of customers. We had thousands of trained telemarketing sales reps and a database of 5,000,000 students. Our strategic advantage was our ability to generate a huge number of customers at a very low cost.

It took KPMG and me three months to put together this comprehensive business plan. It had sophisticated financial modeling, charts, and detailed text that explained every nuance of the business. I decided to name the corporation we were seeking funding for Credit Card Funding Corp. Not a fancy name, to be sure, but one that spelled out clearly what I was planning on doing.

Once we had the business plan complete, KPMG told me I needed to hire an investment banker who could help pitch the deal to several banks with the goal of getting the line of credit to start funding the credit card loans. An investment banker is really a highly trained finance professional who helps business people and corporations put together complex business deals. I was now beginning to see how the financing world actually worked from the bottom up. I would stay up every night studying the words and definitions in a dictionary of financial terms, just to talk the lingo with potential lenders. It was fascinating to expand my knowledge beyond just marketing and sales.

Shopping the Plan

Fortunately, KPMG introduced me to an investment banker who lined up meetings for me with four or five banks. I made appointments with each and, carrying the business plan, tried to interest them in my new company. Their eyes glazed over every time. I'm not sure why, but the consensus seemed to be that I should stick with marketing since that was where my experience had been. They didn't get it, but I didn't get discouraged. I knew eventually we would find someone who believed we could move from marketer to credit card issuer. There was just too much opportunity to give it up.

In the middle of this, Patty told me, in one of our conversations, that the president of Bank Pacific had resigned. I realized that if I could hire a senior executive with years of experience in the credit card business, this might increase my chances of convincing a lender to give me the funding to get started. I told Patty to call him immediately so I could arrange an interview with him. He flew out to California and we talked. It turned out that the main reason he'd quit was to move into something more entrepreneurial. I told him some of what I was trying to do and he got excited. He validated my business plan and I put him on a consulting contract with the understanding that if I were successful in starting the credit card company, he could run it. That was exactly what he wanted to do, and I certainly didn't want to run the business myself.

Part of my hunt for the right bank to provide us with the credit line we needed included researching a member directory from the American Bankers Association. There I found everything from the firms that made the plastic needed for the physical credit cards to the companies generating the credit reports we'd need to determine who got credit cards and who didn't.

> *Don't be afraid to pick up the phone—*
> *over and over again I have found that*
> *just picking up the phone and getting started*
> *can lead to extremely valuable*
> *relationships and business deals.*

One of the organizations in the directory was Bank Data Services. They seemed to handle everything, including underwriting credit card loan applications. As I'd done so many times before, I called them just to see where it would lead, and spoke with a sales representative. He listened and was interested enough to ask me to send him a copy of the business plan. It wasn't long before he called me back, explaining that Bank Data Services was owned by Trust Bank USA, and he thought they might be interested in financing my plan.

Since I was planning to be in the Midwest anyway, I made an appointment with them, not really expecting much to happen. My investment banker joined me and when we walked into their Wisconsin offices we were both astounded. There were fifteen guys in suits, each one high up in Trust Bank USA and Bank Data Services, and each one had in his hands a copy of my business plan. They wanted to know more.

Not only was I able to assure them I could originate at least a million credit cards a year, but I also had the ex-president of Bank Pacific on board. Bank Data Services, of course, wanted the processing end of this business and we told them we'd be much more likely to give them all that business if Trust Bank USA would provide the credit line we needed to finance the credit card loans. Everyone around the table thought it was a winner. Bank Data Services would get all the processing fees, Trust Bank USA would earn interest on our credit line, and Credit Card Funding would get the necessary funds to make the credit card loans. It was a slam-dunk.

Within the week, they came back with a formal proposal—Credit Card Funding Corp. was a go.

It worked. Eventually, we built it out to several hundred million in loans. Trust Bank USA and Bank Data Services generated about $100 million in interest and fees over the course of the relationship. They took a risk on us and were richly rewarded; they thought like entrepreneurs and ended up making a great business deal. It truly was a win/win deal for all of us.

Keep Your Eyes on the Horizon for New Opportunities

Credit Card Funding Corp. is another example of what happens when you keep your eyes open for opportunity. We were able to again leverage our existing expertise just as with the original call center business. Are you starting to see how this pattern repeats itself? You have to continuously step back from the day-to-day business and search for new avenues to expand. If you look long enough and test new concepts, you're bound to find a winner.

9

KNOWING

WHEN

TO SELL

One of the enduring principles of any business is that the environment you are operating in will change drastically, and often in ways that are totally unpredictable. Here we were issuing credit cards by the thousands each and every month. Our strategic advantage—our ability to generate new accounts at an incredibly low rate—continued to work for the first three years, just like clockwork. Then, in 2003, the United States Congress passed legislation that resulted in what today is known as the Do Not Call List Registry. This allowed anyone with a phone number to sign up so they legally could stop product or service solicitations by phone, unless they were already a customer of the soliciting company.

What no one in the credit card industry, ourselves included, anticipated was the fact that well over 75 percent of the households in the country would add their numbers to the Do Not Call list within the first twenty-four months—much higher than anyone had predicted.

In short, the Do Not Call List dramatically reduced the number of calls we could legally make to offer students our credit card. We had lost our strategic advantage.

Fortunately, this didn't happen all at once. We quickly began testing all kinds of other marketing channels. We tried direct mail, e-mail, internet advertising, and on-campus representatives—nothing worked! Our acquisition costs using these methods were just too high. We could have limped along on much less profit, and several of our managers urged us to do just that. They just didn't want to accept the fact that our world had changed.

However, I knew in my gut that when you begin to lose your strategic advantage, either you have to find a new one quickly or your business will start to die. The advent of the Do Not Call list coupled with the ever-present attrition of credit card users told me it was time to sell.

Timing Can Be Everything

It's so tempting to hang on to a business too long. The emotions get involved. It seems that there should be some way to continue to make it work. But you've got to be realistic. When you lose a strategic advantage there's a short period of time when the business is still salable.

I knew that the students who used our credit cards were an attractive group and that many banks would love to have them as customers. After all, soon they would have jobs with decent salaries and would want to buy a car or a home and their level of credit card spending would increase. My hunch was that the major credit card companies would want access to our card holders.

We hired an investment banker and he helped us put together what's known as an "Offering Memorandum." This is a highly detailed document that lays out the financial facts surrounding a business so that a prospective buyer can evaluate it accurately prior to making an offer to buy the company.

As the company had grown, we had become very good at understanding every facet of the credit card business. We developed sophisticated financial models that allowed us to make solid predictions about our cash flow, profitability, losses and growth. We could quickly tell when we needed to change a procedure or process in order to generate additional profit or squeeze down an expense. This allowed us to have absolute clarity about how to optimize the business.

This attention to detail was also the key in finding a buyer for the business. Potential buyers had the opportunity to evaluate the company by more metrics and statistical analysis than offered by most credit card businesses ten times as large.

Eventually, we were successful in selling the business to one of the largest credit card issuers in the country for the exact reasons we anticipated. The buyer wanted access to a highly desirable card holder base that would continue needing credit in the future for products such as auto loans, mortgages and other banking needs.

After the sale of Credit Card Funding Corp., we continued to build Teleservices Direct. Remember that Credit Card

Funding was a separate company focused only on the issuing and financing of credit cards. We still had our large call center operations that provided customer relationship management services to some of the world's largest companies. Since the sale, I have also been investing and building other financial services and real estate companies. But that's another story for another book!

Reasons To Sell a Business

There really are three reasons to sell a business:

- **When you lose your strategic advantage.** Remember, without a strategic advantage a business will begin to slowly lose momentum and value. There is nothing wrong with testing new possible directions or opportunities to replace the lost strategic advantage. However, don't operate with blinders on, if you are not making significant headway; if the business is at risk of losing momentum, it may be a good time to sell. When you hear the alarm bells, you just need to take action, and fast. Listen to your gut and you'll know when you need to sell or change course.

- **When there's a bubble in your industry.** We've all seen it at one time or another. There are periods of time when buyers just get irrational and businesses sell for much more than they are actually worth. I've seen many instances where a buyer has actually paid more for a business than the company will earn over the next fifteen years. That's crazy! If someone offers more than you are going to earn over fifteen years, grab the check with both hands. Don't be surprised; it happens more often that you think.

The only time this rule would not apply is if the business is still growing like crazy, and the future is so predictable that you are assured you will earn more in the long run. This is very rare and you need to be absolutely sure you are not fooling yourself with wishful thinking about the future prospects for the company

- **Personal reasons.** There are all kinds of personal reasons to sell a business. There may be health problems, a change to your family situation, or a desire to change your lifestyle. If you're paying attention to your gut, you'll know when it's time. When it comes to personal reasons, there's no need to try to justify or explain why you're selling the business. There's nothing wrong with simply deciding it's time to get out and the best way to get out is to sell.

A Word About Taking Some Chips off the Table

One of the most valuable lessons I have learned over the years is how important it is to take cash out of a business to diversify your assets any time your business is doing well enough to allow you to do so. Remember, the true value in a business is the cash flow it pays its owner. Many times business owners will reinvest every dollar in a business, only to lose everything if the business hits tough times. You need to realize that a business is usually the owner's largest financial asset, and can be highly illiquid. In order to diversify your assets and net worth, you must take cash distributions and invest them in assets outside the company.

Although I'm a firm believer in reinvesting in your business, it doesn't make sense to put everything back in—at least not forever. Keep in mind, your goal for starting a business is freedom—freedom to do what you want, when you want and the way you want to do it. That kind of freedom takes money. Assuming you're making a decent profit, you've got to let the business stand on its own so that you can start taking large cash distributions. I call this money "Safe Chips." Safe chips are the money you keep "safe" from the risks of the business.

A major reason to protect yourself in this manner is because businesses are full of ups and downs. Saving and investing money protects you against the bumps in the road. If, after some success, your business fails, perhaps because of something you have no control over, your Safe Chips will allow you to develop another business or to continue your lifestyle or both.

I can't tell you the number of times I've seen entrepreneurs succeed, then, when things fell apart, ended up with nothing because they hadn't taken cash out of their business when they could have. In the next couple of chapters we will look at some good rules about investing some of the profits of your business. You may be surprised, but I think the saying "It's easier to make it than to hold on to it" is really true if you don't learn the secrets of protecting the cash you earn from your business.

Investor First; Entrepreneur Second

There is a real art to being a successful business owner. I believe the best way to approach owning a business is to consider yourself an investor first, and an entrepreneur second. You must see yourself as both or the business will own you, instead of you owning the business. What I mean by this is that, when you think of yourself as both, you can separate yourself from running the day-to-day operations.

An investor is a person who invests in a business for a financial return. The investor is not necessarily the business operator. This is a very important distinction. Many investors have no day-to-day oversight of a business. This gives them the opportunity to create and find other investment opportunities. Many times, an investor will hire a CEO to run a company.

Many business owners see themselves only as entrepreneurs, and cannot let go of running the business day to day. In a lot of cases, entrepreneurs get so bogged down in the details of running their business that they have no time or freedom to do anything else. They lose the freedom to spend time with their family and time to just enjoy life. By delegating over time, they can move out of the day-to-day operations and move toward the investor role which allows them much more freedom to pursue other opportunities.

To be truly successful and have the kind of freedom that is possible, you've got to be passionate about your business, but you also have to be able to detach from your business. This may seem contradictory at first, but it really isn't. There's a big difference between being passionate about what you're doing and identifying with it so thoroughly you lose all perspective. Although developing a thriving business is exciting and takes tremendous personal effort, business isn't personal. You are much more than your business. Your business is there to serve you, not the other way around.

If you have to show up every day,
it's a job not a business

That's why I say so often: "Make sure your business doesn't become a job." A job means you have to be there every day. Freedom means just the opposite. Own the business; don't let the business own you. The very best way to do this is to view yourself as an investor first, and entrepreneur second.

10

STARTING A BUSINESS IS THE MOST CERTAIN WAY TO WEALTH

Why is starting a business such a great way to create financial wealth? In order to understand the answer, we must understand what financial wealth is.

Financial wealth is the ability to live comfortably from the income your assets generate.

The name of such an income stream is passive income. Simply, this is income you earn whether you get out of bed in the morning or not.

To see why a business is such a great way to create passive income, we need to do a few simple calculations and compare "earning a salary" from a job with business ownership income.

Let's say you earn a salary, a huge one, of $1,000,000 per year. About half of that million dollars will go to state and federal taxes, so you end up with $500,000 in your pocket. If you saved every penny of that $500K and did the same thing for five years (for simplification I am not including interest or investment income), you would have a savings of $2,500,000. If you wanted to stop working and invested that money in the safest place possible, let's say a United States Certificate of Deposit at 5% interest, you would have "passive" income of $125,000 per year before tax. Remember, in order to accomplish this you had to earn $1 million a year for five years and save every penny of after-tax income.

Let's compare this with starting a business that takes five years to mature, and then generates $1 million a year in earnings before taxes. Meaning, as the owner, you have created $1 million a year in passive income. This is eight times the passive income that the high-salary scenario would generate after the same five years ($1,000,000 versus $125,000).

In other words, it takes massive amounts of personal salary to match the wealth creation of a moderately successful business.

In the example above, you would have to earn several million dollars per year for five years to create the same passive earning stream as the business. This is why so many of the fortunes that have been generated have come from the creators of businesses rather than personal income from a job.

Good vs. Bad Business

While on the subject of why a business is the most certain way to wealth, let's also take a look at what clues can help you differentiate a good business with a high chance of success from a bad business more likely to fail. Earlier in the book we talked about the two most basic criteria for a successful business:

1. A product or service people really want.

2. A very high profit margin.

The two additional criteria I would add in evaluating any business are:

3. The higher the Return on Capital, the better the business opportunity. What does this mean? For every dollar you invest in a business, how much profit will you make? I have seen businesses that generate as high as 20 times invested capital, meaning if you invest $1 million, you can earn $20 million per year. I have also seen businesses that earn nothing on invested capital, meaning they never actually earn money! Profit margin and capital expenditure are the two factors that will determine your Return on Capital ratio.

4. The next factor is scalability. Scalability is the ability of the business to easily expand and grow quickly without physical or capital constraints. For example, many businesses have been able to take advantage of the

Internet to achieve rapid expansion and profit because of relatively low physical and capital costs. The most notable example of this is Google. Google has grown exponentially because of its massive scalability and product offerings that people really want.

When evaluating businesses look for ones with the four criteria above and you will be focused on the most promising opportunities.

11

BUILDING
FINANCIAL WEALTH
OUTSIDE
YOUR BUSINESS OR JOB

While most people want to become wealthy because they want to buy nice things, few realize there is a very practical reason for building wealth. Simply put, both a job or your own business are risky because in each case you're counting on a single source of income to support yourself and your family. Any time you're trusting one income source to keep you going, you are operating in dangerous territory. It is important to understand that businesses large and small fail every day, which means you can lose your income anytime whether or not you own the business. An analogy I like to use is that skydivers never jump with one parachute, they always have a reserve chute. They can pull it if something goes wrong. This strategy should be employed in your personal financial planning as well. In effect, you need to create a reserve parachute to protect yourself and your family in an emergency. That reserve parachute is a passive income stream created from wealth you build for yourself.

Fortunately, there are three simple steps you can take to begin to build wealth so you can diversify your income stream:

Step 1: Budgeting and Saving
Step 2: Controlling Debt
Step 3: Investing

None of this is too complicated; however, it takes tremendous day-to-day discipline in order to stick with the plan. All three steps must be done in parallel for the system of wealth building to work. This is true for the person who makes $20,000 a year as well as for those who make millions a year.

Budgeting

Learning how to budget and disciplining yourself to save is the first key to building wealth. Although not very exciting, budgeting is simply making a plan about spending money, tracking your spending to see if you're close to the plan and making adjustments as needed. Your budget needs to include everything you plan to spend and you need a way to track what you actually spend so you can compare the two. If you've got a business of your own, you'll want a budget for both the business and your personal life.

When coupled with the discipline of savings, you have the beginning of a solid financial plan.

Avoid the Lifestyle Treadmill

Don't let yourself fall into the trap of getting on what I call the "Lifestyle Treadmill." The Lifestyle Treadmill means that you never start to save money because every time you start to earn more money you increase your living expenses. It's okay to slowly increase your spending if you are making significant progress in your savings and investing efforts; however, that is not usually what happens.

The typical scenario is that a person doubles their income but their lifestyle expenses triple or more. It usually starts with expensive cars and trips, then progresses to a big house and toys like jets and vacation homes. When this happens, the person on the Lifestyle Treadmill has to run faster and faster to keep earning enough to maintain their lifestyle and usually ends up crashing from a problem in their job or business. They have no financial reserves and in the worst scenario go broke or file bankruptcy. Don't let that happen to you. I am all for buying nice things, but don't increase your lifestyle without always first setting aside your "Safe Chips" for investing and savings.

Savings Is a Way of Taking Some Chips off the Table

A savings account is a first step in getting some of your chips off the table. This will start you on the road to investing and will be your first line of defense if your income from your business or job is temporarily affected. Savings are your safety net.

How much should you save? At a minimum, ten percent of your after-tax income will work. If, at the moment, you can't put that much away, work toward it. As your income increases, make sure your savings percentage increases too. If you make it a habit to pull savings from every paycheck or every source of income as it comes in, you'll start to build a good asset base.

Your goal is having at least six months of living expenses (which you know because of your budget) in a savings account. A full year is even better. Once you've got your cushion, you can begin to invest.

Controlling Debt

There's nothing wrong with debt as long as it's the kind of debt that can help you create income or finance an asset that has appreciation potential. On the other hand, most consumer debt, including credit card debt—is terrible, and can easily bury you financially. The two factors that make most consumer debt reckless are:

1. Most consumer debt has a very high interest associated with it, and,

2. Most consumer debt is used to finance a purchase that will go down in value.

Almost everything you buy—including automobiles, electronics and appliances—is worth much less than what you pay for it immediately after you bring it home. If you are also paying interest to own it, this means you are financing a purchase that is losing value every day. Don't get yourself in this situation.

For example, if you owe $10,000 in credit card debt at 18 percent interest and make payments of $250 per month, it will take you 62 months (just over five years) to pay it off, assuming you don't charge another nickel. As if that's not bad enough, by the time you've paid it off you'll have paid a total of $15,500! That's $5,500 more than your original $10,000. Even worse is the stuff you finally paid off is probably now worth next to nothing! That's why you should pay off your credit cards in full each and every month—it's just too costly not to. And if you have gotten into a situation where you can't pay them off every month, stop spending until you can.

Obviously, I'm not opposed to credit cards, but I am suggesting they should be paid off in full each and every month. In fact, I'll go so far as saying don't charge anything unless you're sure you can pay for it the same month you buy it. That's the only way to use credit cards and avoid the huge interest fees.

Debt as Leverage

Just to be clear, debt—properly used—can help you leverage your cash to more profit. Debt can actually be a tool to make more money. For example, you could borrow money in the form of a mortgage to own a rental house. Chances are if you sell that house in five or ten years from your date of purchase, you'll make a profit and the rental income will pay all the interest on the mortgage.

Rule of thumb: use leverage only to buy an asset that's going to increase in value.

Investing

Once you've got around a year's worth of savings, it's time to start investing so your money starts working for you rather than the other way around. Investing is a very important subject and should be studied in depth in order to really have a good understanding of all the opportunities and pitfalls. There are, however, a few broad guidelines I want to share with you.

Cash

About 50 percent of your liquid investment dollars should go into secure Certificates of Deposit and/or money market investments. The other half should go into equities, stocks and income producing real estate. In other words, if you have $100,000 to invest, roughly $50,000 would go into CDs and money market funds, $25,000 into stocks and $25,000 into real estate. This may sound like a very high allocation of cash holdings, however, I believe having a very large reserve of cold, hard cash gives you the flexibility to take advantage of opportunities that might arise quickly. You may go from 50 percent cash to 30 percent, based on a good investment opportunity, but always target building your cash reserve back up to around 50 percent. As I have said earlier, "Cash Is King," meaning it gives you power, flexibility and freedom.

Index Funds

When it comes to investing in stocks, here is an astonishing fact. More than 75 percent of the professional mutual fund money managers can't beat the market averages, which are indexes like the Dow Jones Industrials and Standard and Poor's 500. This means if you can just track how the overall stock market does you will beat the returns of 75 percent of the professional mutual fund managers. To do this, you can just buy index funds that track right with the averages. You'll pay much less in fees and your returns will be higher than most of the mutual fund managers'. There are very few investors in the entire world who have proven track records of beating the market averages over time. Usually if they do, it's by taking huge risks. I firmly believe you will do much better just holding globally diverse index funds. This will guarantee you the lowest cost and beat the majority of actively managed funds. There is a lot to learn about the stock market, mutual funds, and other investments, so it is really important to read books and take investment classes so you thoroughly understand how financial markets work.

Income Producing Real Estate

Income producing real estate, such as rental homes, apartments or commercial buildings, can make fantastic long term investments. Real estate offers many tax benefits and also can easily be financed using a mortgage to create high returns from the financial leverage you gain. But remember, real estate isn't as liquid as stocks. This is why you only want to make it a portion of your investments. That said, real estate, properly chosen and held over a long period of time, can often be the foundation of a fortune. Again, spend time learning all you can about real estate investing, as it is the most common way to build a high net worth from investing.

Compounding

The sooner you start saving and investing the better. The

reason for this is what's known as compounding. Compounding means to make money on both your investment and the interest on your investment. So you are making money on a constantly growing asset base.

That explanation doesn't really make clear the almost magical quality of compounding interest. To best understand compounding, you need to understand what's known as the Compounding Rule of 72. The rule gives you a way to determine how long it will take you to double your money. Simply take the number, 72, and divide it by any annual percentage return rate and you'll get your answer. For example, if you are earning 9 percent, just divide 72 by 9 and you'll discover it takes 8 years to double your money; at 15% it will take almost 5 years.

It gets better. If you invest $50,000 at 15%, in five years it will be worth over $100,000; almost half a million in 15 years, and over $1.6 million in 25 years—that's 32 times your initial investment. Obviously, the sooner you get started, the better. If you are young and even have a small amount to invest, you can build a huge fortune just by letting compounding work for you.

Avoid Getting Ripped Off

There are two common mistakes you want to avoid on your wealth building voyage. The first is being suckered into buying investment products with very high fees and the second is falling for investment scams.

High Fee Investment Products

As an investor you will no doubt be approached over and over by salespeople disguised as investment advisors. They will try to sell you inferior products with outrageous fees and expenses. Many investment and insurance products have huge fees buried inside them. You must get educated to spot not only these products, but also the people pushing them.

As you begin to build your investment portfolio, ask one of your trusted mentors to introduce you to an investment advisor who strictly provides advice but does not earn commissions from selling you investment or insurance products. There are excellent "Advice Only" advisors who can help educate you about low cost, high quality investment products. Education is the key to protecting yourself. Learn as much as possible about investing through classes, books, advisors and mentors. By educating yourself you will avoid many of the pitfalls that can be devastating to your net worth.

Ponzi or Private Money Schemes

A Ponzi scheme is a fraudulent investment operation that involves paying super high returns by stealing money from one investor to pay another their profits. In the end, there is no money to pay all the investors since the profits were fake. It's really just a scam so that the promoters can steal money for themselves. It's named after a notorious criminal of the 1920's named Charles Ponzi, who stole millions of dollars running a scheme like this.

The way to avoid a Ponzi scheme—be cautious of any investment that emphasizes:

1. Extremely high yield returns. If it sounds too good to be true, it usually is.
2. A complex business that you really don't understand.

3. The chance to get in on a "once in a lifetime opportunity."

4. Lastly, and the most important red flag, never invest money with an investment advisor who does not use a globally respected brokerage firm registered with the Securities and Exchange Commission (SEC) as a custodian for your assets. Invest only through very well known investment houses, such as Bank of America, Schwab, Fidelity, Merrill Lynch, etc. In other words, never invest by writing a check to a friend, acquaintance or company where the custodian isn't a large global financial institution. I have seen several sophisticated investors lose millions by investing in private investment partnerships that ended up being Ponzi schemes. Stick with financial institutions that have a fiduciary responsibility to make sure the investments they offer are legitimate.

A Word on Philanthropy and Charitable Giving

I have found that getting involved with a non-profit organization is a great way to give back to your community, and you'll feel great about yourself too. The important thing to know about charities is that they will take your time and money or both.

If you're just starting out and still setting up your investing program, you are better off giving some time and expertise to a non-profit organization. Once you have a solid foundation of assets, it's okay to give more money than time. Pick organizations that you really have a passion for. Meet the leaders of the organization and make sure the money you give is truly being utilized efficiently.

You'll be surprised that you will not only feel great by helping a charitable cause, but you will also meet other interesting people. Most successful people tend to "give back," and getting involved with non-profit organizations is great way to meet other like-minded contacts.

Wealth Building in a Nutshell

There you have it, wealth building in a nutshell. By learning and using these three steps:

1. Budgeting and Saving
2. Controlling Debt
3. Investing

you'll have a formula that works no matter how much you have. The program works for those making minimum wage and it works well for those making millions.

When you use these three steps and avoid the mistakes we have discussed, you'll find your money will soon be working for you instead of you working for money.

12

THE THREE CORNERSTONES
OF SUCCESS

In order to succeed beyond ordinary accomplishments in any endeavor, you will need to build a strong foundation using what I call the Three Cornerstones of Success.

1. Belief

2. Goals/Organization

3. Good Habits

I call them the Three Cornerstones because I have never seen anyone achieve consistent and outstanding performance in areas such as business, science, sports or even philanthropy without honing their skills in the three cornerstones. Let's explore each.

Belief

Ultimately, anyone who truly succeeds in any endeavor has the ability to take a leap of faith. They are able to make a decision, to take a risk, without knowing how it will turn out. They know they can transform their life, their business and even themselves without being able to see the exact results in advance.

Here is an easy way to visualize what I am talking about. Most people tend to be afraid to go out and pursue a far-reaching goal because they really don't know the exact route to take to get there. The secret is that extraordinary achievements cannot be mapped out the way you plan a trip across the country in your car. Anyone with a map can drive across country because each turn and road has already been mapped and explored before.

In life, not all your achievements are going to be pre-mapped so, in a sense, you have to be comfortable driving without a map and clear directions for every turn. Get comfortable building belief that you will find your way by using your gut instincts, knowledge, mentors and other rules and tools we have discussed so far.

When you start a business or do anything else a bit out of the ordinary, you don't have the ability to get a map that will give you every twist and turn. You probably can't even see your destination clearly. Yet, if you're going to be successful, you must have the faith to start, and to continue, even though you don't quite see where you're going or how to get there.

The kind of belief I'm talking about is a sense of destiny. It will take self-confidence and a burning desire to pursue a goal. In order to build the self-confidence and belief you will need in the pursuit of your goals, you will literally need to program your mind for success. The reason for this is all ideas, goals and plans develop in your mind's eye.

There are many great quotes that sum up this philosophy

such as "As you think, so shall you become" (Bruce Lee) and "What I can conceive and believe, I can achieve" (John Smart, Julie Doherty, Stephen L. Nelson). Probably the best book to help understand this kind of belief is *Think and Grow Rich* by Napoleon Hill. Even though it was written back in the late 1930's, it's a classic that you need to read and keep in your library to read over and over again. This book will teach you how to literally train your mind for success. For seventy years, many of the most successful people in the world have pointed to this book as their launch point to success. I cannot emphasize enough the value of what this book teaches. The more you reread this book and follow the philosophy, the stronger your mind will become.

I was lucky to discover this book at one of the toughest periods of my business career and it immediately helped me change my mindset and outlook. In a very short time I had turned what looked like a huge failure into a success by following the principles outlined in the book.

Goals/Organization

Goal setting and organization make up the second cornerstone to success. In its simplest form, goal setting is organizing your life to achieve results in the most efficient way possible. If you can learn how to set goals and achieve them, you will also be getting highly organized as well. Organization and goal setting are vital ingredients for success.

First, let's take a look at a real-world example of organization in action.

You can see the value of organization by considering how airline pilots perform their duties. Commercial airline pilots have achieved a tremendous safety record while operating complex aircraft and transporting millions of people each year. In fact, the airline industry is one of the safest industries in the world. In large measure, that success is because every single procedure each pilot performs is planned and organized. There are checklists for everything, beginning with walking around the outside of the aircraft to visually inspect the engines and wings prior to every flight, to reviewing a long checklist inside the cockpit with the co-pilot, which includes fuel requirements, weather, flight plan and other critical components of each flight. Every move is planned and every contingency planned for, all in support of the goal of getting the airplane from point A to point B safely. Can you imagine if pilots just jumped in and fired up the engines without any organized planning? The safety record would be a disaster and no one would have the confidence to fly.

You can see by this example, just the discipline of being highly organized can make a huge impact on any endeavor.

An example of goal setting on a global scale was the United States' goal of putting a man on the moon. In 1961 then President John F. Kennedy challenged the nation to **"...commit itself to achieving the goal, before this decade is out, of landing a man on the Moon and returning him safely..."** Once the clearly stated goal of putting a man on the moon by 1970 was articulated, all the individuals who were involved in the space program, and, in fact much of the country, had a clear mission to achieve. That clear goal created a massive coordinated effect that led to Neil Armstrong walking on the moon eight years later. The accomplishment never would have been achieved without a clearly defined goal and a list of steps to achieve them.

You can use these same tools, goal setting and organization, to achieve similarly outstanding results. It's really not difficult. For example if, every Sunday evening, you put together a list of five goals you want to accomplish during the next week, by the end of the year you would have accomplished 260 mini-goals. That's huge! I guarantee if you can accomplish that many goals a year, you are on your way to major success. Make sure these weekly goals are not a typical "to do" list such as do laundry or go to grocery store. Instead, make sure the goals you set count for something and move you toward what you really want in life.

I set goals in eight key areas. The reason for these eight is they help keep me as balanced as possible, by making sure I am focused on all key areas of my life. The eight areas are:

1. Health
2. Business/financial
3. Fun
4. Family
5. Charity
6. Community
7. Spiritual
8. Friendship

Each year I take time to establish a major goal for the year in each of the eight areas. Then, each week I set up my schedule and activities to make sure I am on track to achieve them.

Designing Your Own Goal Setting Program

Goal setting is a very personal process. Each person should figure out the optimal goal setting program for themselves. I recommend reading The Power of Focus: How to Hit Your Business, Personal and Financial Targets with Absolute Certainty by Jack Canfield, Mark Victor Hanson and Les Hewitt. This book has an expanded section on goal setting and has a great template to set up your own goal-setting program.

At a minimum, start setting weekly goals every Sunday night and you will be amazed at your results. Without clearly defined goals, you are just wandering without any sense of direction. Goal setting sets your course.

Good Habits

The third cornerstone is what I call Good Habit Creation. Habits create long term results in your life. Good habits can help you maintain your health, create wealth, build strong friendships and family bonds, while bad habits can create sickness, destructive behavior, poverty, etc. Your habits control your destiny, so make them as positive as possible.

The Three Week Rule

One of the amazing things about human nature is the fact that if you do anything, good or bad, for about three weeks, you form a habit. As a result of that three-week practice you'll find it easy to continue performing that activity.

You can use the same principle to let go of bad habits, even, in many cases, addiction. True, you may need some extra support for some problems, and if you do, don't hesitate to get it, but you'll find the three-week rule holds true even if you need some help. Knowing it takes only three weeks to establish a positive behavior or rid yourself of a destructive habit makes it easy to discipline yourself.

With this in mind, get a piece of paper and make a list of good habits that would make your life better. This list can be very simple such as:

Working out
Goal setting
Eating a healthy diet

Commit to making yourself stick to these new habits and you will be amazed after three weeks how easy it is to make these good habits permanent. Then make a list of your bad habits and eliminate them for three weeks also. You will again see it is much easier to stop permanently at that point. Every month or so, spend the time to revisit your habits and continue to optimize by creating good habits while eliminating bad ones.